24 HOURS IN THE LIFE OF LOS ANGELES

LINDA WOLF

ARTHUR TRESS

24 HOURS IN THE LIFE OF

LOS ANGELES

EDITED BY KLAUS FABRICIUS & RED SAUNDERS

INTRODUCTION BY CAROL SCHWALBERG • TEXT BY WANDA COLEMAN & JEFF SPURRIER

ALFRED VAN DER MARCK EDITIONS NEW YORK

THIS BOOK IS DEDICATED TO OUR FAMILIES, OUR FRIENDS, AND OUR LOVED ONES FOR THEIR SUPPORT THROUGHOUT THIS PROJECT.

FRONT COVER PHOTO: PETER LAVERY
BACK COVER PHOTO: CRAIG DIETZ, RED SAUNDERS,
SCOTT BROCK & WILL WHITE
INSERT PHOTO: RENE BURRI/MAGNUM

Library of Congress Cataloging in Publication Data
Main entry under title:

24 hours in the life of Los Angeles.

1. Los Angeles (Calif.)—Social conditions—Pictorial works. 2. Los Angeles (Calif.)—Description—Views. I. Fabricius, Klaus, 1947– . II. Saunders, Red, 1945– . III. Coleman, Wanda. IV. Spurrier, Jeff, 1947– . V. Title: Twenty-four hours in the life of Los Angeles.
HN80.L7A55 779'.9979494053 84-50571
ISBN 0-912383-04-6
ISBN 0-912383-03-8 (pbk.)

FIRST PRINTING JUNE 1984

COLOR SEPARATIONS BY TERRY HARSTAD/TH GRAPHICS
TYPOGRAPHY BY TAURUS, INC., PHOTOTYPOGRAPHERS

PRINTED & BOUND BY R.R. DONNELLEY AND SONS COMPANY
IN THE UNITED STATES OF AMERICA

ALFRED VAN DER MARCK EDITIONS
235 PARK AVENUE SOUTH SUITE 407 NEW YORK, NEW YORK 10003

EDITORS: KLAUS FABRICIUS, RED SAUNDERS

CO-ORDINATOR: ROBERT WALTER

PROJECT DIRECTOR: RED SAUNDERS

ASSOCIATE PRODUCER: TONY CARDOZA

ASSOCIATE CREATIVE DIRECTOR: MIKE DOUD

DESIGN AND ART DIRECTION: SYD SHELTON, RED SAUNDERS

DESIGN CONSULTANT: NANCY STEINY

ART PRODUCTION MANAGER: JIM De LOUISE

TEXT EDITOR: CAROL SCHWALBERG

PRODUCTION SUPERVISOR: SUE READY

PRODUCTION: P.L. diCORCIA, WILL WHITE

PRODUCTION ADMINISTRATION AND LOCATIONS: TEVIS RUNYAN, DAN BORRIS

PRODUCTION ASSISTANTS: BEVERLY KORENWASER, LIZBETH WILLIAMSON
BILL HAYES, LAURA STUART

COMPUTER CONSULTANT: SCOTT BROCK

TRANSPORTATION: JASON NEU

MARKETING: BRUCE ANDERSON, MARY BALLETTA

BUSINESS, FINANCIAL & LEGAL OPERATIONS: KLAUS FABRICIUS, IMTIAZ ARIAN

CONSULTANT ADVISORS: DAVID FAHEY (G. RAY HAWKINS GALLERY), ALICE GEORGE (FORTUNE MAGAZINE)
WOLFGANG BEHNKEN (STERN MAGAZINE), APRIL SILVER (ESQUIRE MAGAZINE), ELLEN MADERE (ESQUIRE MAGAZINE)
LAURIE KRATOCHVIL (ROLLING STONE MAGAZINE), PATRICIA STRATHERN (PARIS)

EVENT PUBLIC RELATIONS: RON BARON, JUSTIN PIERCE (NORMAN WINTER & ASSOCIATES)

PROJECT PUBLIC RELATIONS: FRAN ZONE (CARL BYOIR & ASSOCIATES, INC.)

BUSINESS ANALYSIS PROGRAM: DALE SCHLATHER

L.A. PHOTOGRAPHIC SPONSORS: A&I (E6 COLOR PROCESSING), P.R.S. (PHOTO EQUIPMENT FILMS SERVICES)
PHOTO IMPACT (B&W PROCESSING & CONTACTS)

PROJECT TRAVEL AGENTS: STUDENT TRAVEL NETWORK (U.S.A., EUROPE & AUSTRALIA)

SECURITY: DALLAS GORDON

OFFICIAL PHOTOGRAPHIC CONSULTANT: EASTMAN KODAK COMPANY

FINANCIAL CONSULTANTS: STATHAM DUFF STOOP (CITY OF LONDON)

SPECIAL THANKS TO GARETH ROBERTSON WITHOUT WHOSE HELP THE BOOK WOULD NOT HAVE BEEN POSSIBLE.

LAVERY

Forget geography, junk the globe. The tourist guides are telling the truth: The real crossroads of the world is here, Hollywood and Vine, the heart of that endless suburb, that hodge podge of cities, mountains, beaches, and desert called the Greater Metropolitan Los Angeles area.

Six hundred bucks will buy a round trip ticket to London or Hong Kong. Los Angeles stands at the midpoint between Old World and Third World, the fulcrum between East and West, North and South.

LINDA WOLF

It is a city of enormous wealth and power. People earn more money and spend more money than anywhere else, and most draw their pay from either the war factory whose products can destroy the world or the dream factory whose images beguile the world and glue over two billion eyes to the television screen.

In the beginning there was no reason for Los Angeles to be there — no harbor, no minerals, no meeting of trade routes, no commanding view. The site amounted to a semi-arid plain, watered by a meandering stream and separated from the desert and chaparral beyond by a ring of eroded mountains.

Yet the tiny settlement of 44 people that began two centuries ago as El Pueblo de Nuestra Señora la Reina de los Angeles de Porciuncula burgeoned into Greater Los Angeles, a city that became the ultimate style setter in fads, fitness, and junk food, and today's forecaster of the way everyone will live tomorrow.

To this vast megalopolis, in March 1984, came 100 talented photographers from France, England, Ireland, Germany, Austria, Switzerland, Czechoslovakia, Italy, India, Australia, and Japan, all parts of the United States, and the City of Angels itself. Some had credits that filled four typewritten pages, and some were just starting out. What lured them was a unique project: to freeze forever 24 hours in the life of Los Angeles, to create a photographic time capsule that would go beyond the glitter of Tinseltown, the wealth of Bel-Air, and the freakiness of Hollywood to reveal the normal everyday life of Los Angeles, people eating, drinking, working, playing, partying, walking, driving, and eventually, like the exhausted but exhilarated photographers, dropping off to sleep.

Since Hollywood images have made Los Angeles everyone's second home, photographers who had never set foot here still experienced *déja vu*. They had watched *Kojak* in Polish and Bob Hope in Spanish. After seeing *Chips*, they could recognize the Pacific Coast Highway and Rayban sunglasses when they saw them.

VOLKER HINZ

For the American contingent and particularly the local photographers, the special excitement came from the idea of the time frame, and the challenge of looking at the city as an outsider.

A brief digression. Photographers are known to be blasé, jaded, and as jealous of their own assignments as a mother lion defending a cub. This time, cooperation burst into full bloom. Los Angeles photographers brainstormed lists of likely subjects. Others met on their own to parcel out work. "Say, if you're covering bikers, maybe I should do mud wrestling." Everyone brimmed with energy and nervous tension.

Added to the professionals was a crew of local schoolchildren, who were handed Kodak Disc cameras and then instructed to go out and have fun taking pictures.

Less than six weeks after the project directors set up shop, less than six weeks after hectic planning of flights, rooms, car rentals, film, assistants, clearances, and hundreds of other details, the photographers fanned out over the Los Angeles basin. They began a minute after midnight Friday, March 30, 1984 and returned 24 hours later with 1,200,000 images. From that number, an international team of editors culled the selection you see in this book.

Sprawl was the first reality confronting

the photographers. They were roaming over an area half the size of Belgium. Speed and speed alone would conquer this space. That meant cars. In Los Angeles, taxis come only by appointment, and only the very old, the very young, the poor, and the mentally ill ride the wheezing buses. The pink slip, the certificate of car ownership, is the umbilical cord connecting an Angeleno to the world. An ailing car can mean disaster. When a friend was told that Tom's father was sick and perhaps dying, she took it with a perfunctory uh-huh, but when the brakes went out on my car, she moaned in commiseration, "Oh, man!"

Angelenos love their cars and bestow friendly nicknames like bug or T-bird, Vette or Jag. The weekly wash-and-wax takes on the sanctity of attendance at mass, while a devoted Porsche owner will mask the hood with a leather "bra" to keep off bugs. Encapsulated in a car with the windows rolled up, the air conditioner on, and the tape deck playing, the Angeleno experiences a surge of power. "By God, I can go anywhere!"

People feel free to slip into Los Angeles for a few years and then slip out again. Even those who stay move often. With the average apartment tenancy coming to less than a year, the prudent use pencil in their address books.

Los Angeles ranks as the entertainment capital of the world. People on six continents held their breath for months to find out who shot J.R., and Charlton Heston signs as many autographs in Hong Kong as in Hollywood.

Movies may not be better than ever, but they are back raking in profits. Just when cinematic Jeremiahs were prophesying the demise of the movie business, directors drew on the high tech skills native to Los Angeles to produce *Jaws, Star Wars, Close Encounters of the Third Kind,* and *E.T.* Such blockbusters excited the investors and proved that reports of the industry's death were greatly exaggerated.

Los Angeles, the city that gave you The Doors, Joni Mitchell, and Randy Newman, is still the mecca of recording. Even Motown, America's most famous and powerful black recording company, uprooted itself from Detroit because, in the music business, Los Angeles is the Big Orange. Big companies still favor the safer mainstream pop tunes, but thanks to the influence of independent labels, local bands like X, the GoGos, the Blasters, and Latino-flavored Los Lobos "break through to the other side" from Los Angeles to the world.

Show biz gives Los Angeles its special glitz, and nearly everyone goes Hollywood. Bikers are movie extras playing bikers.

TOM VINETZ

Children play with larger-than-life Disney dolls. A secretary whose second cousin is a third-string villain on television confides the name of her plastic surgeon.

As glamour capital, Los Angeles is pre-occupied with beauty and fitness. Probably no other city has a greater density of plastic surgeons, exercise salons, and nail wrappers. Dinner guests discuss the benefits of colon therapy and isolation tanks. As they debate jogging versus weight lifting, words like deltoid and polyglycerides come trippingly to the tongue. If Los Angeles ever adopted a coat-of-arms, it would show two joggers rampant on a field of alfalfa shoots.

Mother's milk to many is drugs. In Los Angeles, anything goes better with coke, or H, angel dust, China whites, PCP, ludes. Of the soft drugs, cannabis is now the biggest cash crop in California, and many canny indoor agriculturists harvest marijuana seven times a year thanks to hydroponics and floodlights 24 hours a day.

For all its pervasiveness, show biz hires fewer people than aerospace. Lockheed, TRW, McDonnell-Douglas, and Hughes Aircraft combined employ 128,000 workers, or enough people to fill two Santa Fes. Aerospace and weapons mean big bucks in Southern California.

Whether they work in movies, aerospace,

oil, or agriculture, most adult Angelenos come from somewhere else. Cut adrift from family and roots, they throw off the constraints of tradition and good taste that might stop them from trying new ideas. There is nothing to keep an artist from painting a poem on a wall, a swimsuited salesman from plunging into a tank to demonstrate an underwater camera housing, or the ultra-rich from hiring a helicopter with tuxedoed pilot and cordon bleu meal.

This willingness to try new ideas has made Los Angeles the city of the second chance, the place where a struggling English teacher from Cleveland becomes a wealthy manufacturer of aircraft parts, where an uneducated Irish laborer rises to chief engineer on the Owens Valley project, and where a lifeguard-cum-radio announcer turns first actor, then governor, and finally President of the United States.

Since Los Angeles never stops growing, this expansion alone breeds wealth. The average annual income runs ahead of the national figures. Money is the bottom line and a constant preoccupation. As thou earnest, so shalt thou be judged. Druggists and dentists join rock stars in the search for the ultimate tax shelter.

The actual shelters are flimsier. Despite prices that can run 50 percent higher than elsewhere in the country, these houses come sans basement, sans expandable attic, sans central heating, and often sans insulation. A building contractor once explained why he preferred putting up houses in Los Angeles: "Anything I can't get away with in New York or Atlanta, I ship out here."

Some of these shacks are splendid indeed, Los Angeles versions of Tudor cottages, Norman chateaux, and Mexican haciendas, and they can fetch prices in the millions. If you've got it, flaunt it. Dig a pool, add bathrooms, and don't forget the sauna and Jacuzzi. Oh, yes, remodel the kitchen, and hire a decorator. No one with money decorates without professional guidance.

Beyond the flimsy, even oddball, architecture lies a terrain of great natural appeal. As Wanda Coleman noted in her poem, *Prisoner of Los Angeles,*

my eyes capture the purple reach
  of hollywood's hills
the gold eye of sun mounting the east
the gray anguished arms of avenue
i will never leave here

In stunning contrast to the million dollar mansions are the barrios where three families may cram into a single room and a skid row with the biggest collection of down-and-outers of any American city. Every day hundreds line up at missions for free meals.

DENNIS DARLING

The poverty is not evenly spread. At press time, California unemployment for whites was seven percent, but the figure zoomed to 12 percent among Latinos and 16 percent among blacks.

Such facts are not visible to most whites because of de facto segregation. Latinos tend to cluster in East Los Angeles and blacks in Watts and south-central Los Angeles. The law now forbids discrimination in housing, and wealthier blacks and Latinos may live anywhere they can afford the price, but when Los Angeles attempted to integrate city schools by busing white students to minority neighborhoods, their parents planted their young in private institutions.

The middle class ignores these facts and revels in a dogged pursuit of pleasure, forever taking off to the beach or the desert and turning any occasion into a picnic. After observing an audience at the Hollywood Bowl, a German journalist fumed, "This isn't a concert. It's just eating with music."

Should hedonism pall, Angelenos can peruse a menu of spiritual delights. Catholics, Protestant, Greek Orthodox, and Jews observe their faiths here as everywhere, but attendance at services is lower. Many people recommend a guru as they might a hairdresser, and yogis offer exercise along with insight. While American Sikhs might not play in Peoria, they ruffle no feathers in Los Angeles.

Some worship before the TV set. Religion has its own channel in Los Angeles, a city that outdoes all others in viewing hours. The addicted may find 15 channels on television, some with programs in Spanish, Japanese, and Korean, and 21 on cable.

Long before television, the Gabrielino Indians roamed the area. Like later settlers, they were accused of sloth, indecency,

HORST WACKERBARTH

unimpressive housing, and smog.

The first Mexican settlers took one look at the black, loamy soil and realized that if they poked a stick into it and watered well, it would bear fruit. By producing wine, beef, and lamb for all of California, the rancheros prospered. In 1870, when drought ruined the cattle business and the wool boom collapsed, Los Angeles struck gold in the shape of the navel orange. Later, wealth would come with oil, movies and plane fabrication, to say nothing of the land itself. Real estate promoters carved up vacant acreage and created entire towns like Santa Monica and Venice.

But huge growth required harbors and water. After annexing the ports of Wilmington and San Pedro, Los Angeles ordered a 200-mile aqueduct to the Owens River, and, with water as a weapon, gobbled up neighboring communities.

Racism reared its head several times, most notably during the Zoot Suit riots against Latinos in 1942 and in the Watts riots 23 years later.

Despite hundreds of thousands of Latinos, Japanese, and Native Americans, the city remained essentially bland and blonde until the 70s. All the children seemed to be towheads, and the only people speaking foreign languages were Mexican maids and Japanese gardeners.

As the photographs show, world events caught up with Los Angeles. The end of the Vietnam war, the fall of the Shah of Iran, and conflict in Lebanon and Central America brought in thousands of Nicaraguans, Salvadoreans, Armenians, Vietnamese. Today, Korean signs dominate long stretches of Olympic Boulevard, and city schools report students speak over 100 languages other than English. Los Angeles is no longer a typical, cornfed American town.

The presence of so many Asians provides an important Asian connection. Los Angeles now considers itself a city on the Pacific Rim, a meeting place of Orient and Occident. And well it might, for most Japanese firms have established their American base in Southern California, and more Asian goods enter the country through the port of Los Angeles/Long Beach than any other harbor.

CHRISTOPHER MAKOS

Equally important is the bridge to the South. Every fourth person in Los Angeles County is Latino, and Latino children now make up half the student body in city schools. An estimated two million *undocumentados* have fled the poverty of Mexico and the strife of Central America to *El Norte*. For many, the promise of Los Angeles outstrips the reality. Illegals often work at less than minimum wage, yet those who staff restaurant kitchens and garment industry sweatshops count themselves well off compared to those who find no work at all.

The night before the shoot, rain fell. When it stopped, wind from the desert swept away the smog. It was a dream of a day, the kind tourist folders promise and photographers pray for.

Most worked the full 24 hours. It became a total experience, a photographic event. It is that tension, that edge, that spontaneity that the book is about. What the photographers hoped to accomplish was not a comprehensive view of Los Angeles — 1,000 photographers could shoot for 24 days and not cover everything — but a searing look at North, South, East, and West; L.A.'s worst, L.A.'s best. Turn these pages, and check it out.

Is trouble brewing in Paradise, or will Los Angeles luck out once more?

ANDREW MOORE

As the new day begins in Wilmington, the only sounds are barking dogs and trucks passing on the Harbor Freeway. In the distance, the lights of the Naval Fuel Reserve burn. For photographer Andrew Moore, the scene is surreal: "The strangeness of palm trees amidst this smoky brilliance. The world of night revealed."

GERED MANKOWITZ

MOSHE BRAKHA

At Selma and Vine, these bikers and mamas, who are also movie extras, ponder whether tis nobler to suffer rousts by Hollywood police or pay dues and join the Screen Actors Guild.

Left: Touted as a luxurious relaxation center, Le Hot Tub Club in West Hollywood has everything from free local limousine service to 18 fantasy suites, rented on an hourly basis, with "dermo-controlled" Jacuzzis.

GERED MANKOWITZ

WILLIAM KLEIN

Members of The Luminaires, a women's support group of the Estelle Doheny Eye Foundation, enjoy a fund raiser at the Sheraton Grande Hotel in downtown.

Left: Waiters at Joe Allen, a Los Angeles branch of a New York restaurant, leave work in the early morning.

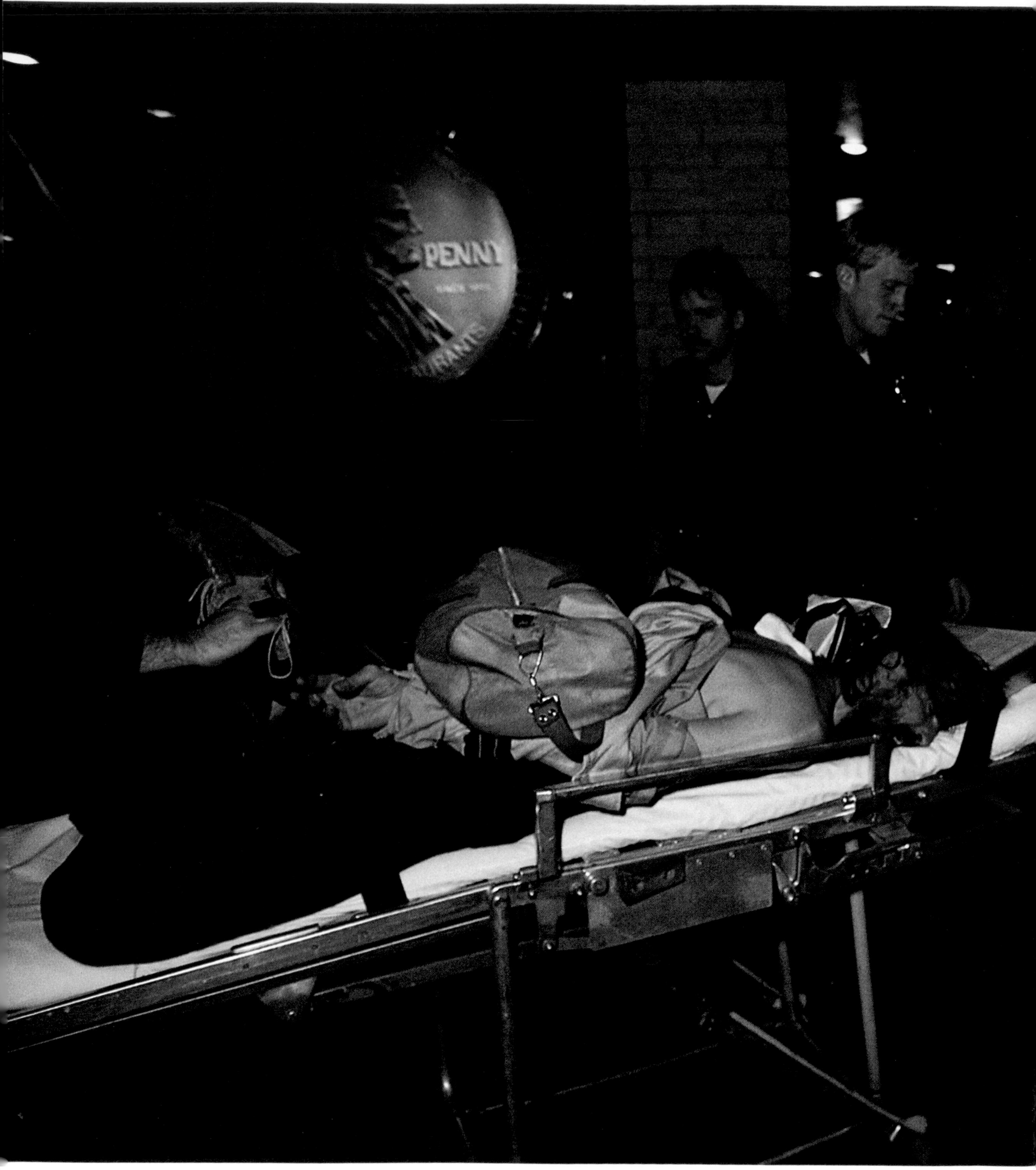

PENNY

A young man with a mental illness record is subdued by police outside the Copper Penny coffee shop in Hollywood after he became violent. "Big cities all have areas where people who can't take care of themselves drift to," explained a worker for the Los Angeles County Mental Health Department. Skid row and Hollywood are two areas that receive more than their share of such transients. A representative for the Hollywood Mental Health Service facility estimates that there are up to 2,000 severely disabled former mental patients in Hollywood. Adding to the problem are recent budget cutbacks in both state and Federal programs, which forced local hospital wards and out-patient clinics to limit their services.

DAN ESGRO

6:45 A.M. Mr Goldstein to schul - Fairfax area

7.20 A.M. Sam works at IRV's newsstand - Fairfax

7.45 am Beverly Hills Policeman.

7.55 A.M Bev Hills waiting for hair appointment

8:00 A.M Rodeo Collection Beverly Hills

8:05 A.M Rodeo Collection Beverly Hills

8.36 A.M. Don & a Friend

8.38 A.M. Bev Hills Maid and Gardener

8.40 A.M. Beverly Hills

12:30pm Mom – Bev Hills

12:00 Patrick Terrail Ma Maison

12:40pm Mail Lady – Bev hills

3:30pm Charlie Simmer L.A. KINGS & baby Brittany with wife Terri Welles Playmate of the year 1980.

5.05pm Laura Huxley & Goddaughter Karen.

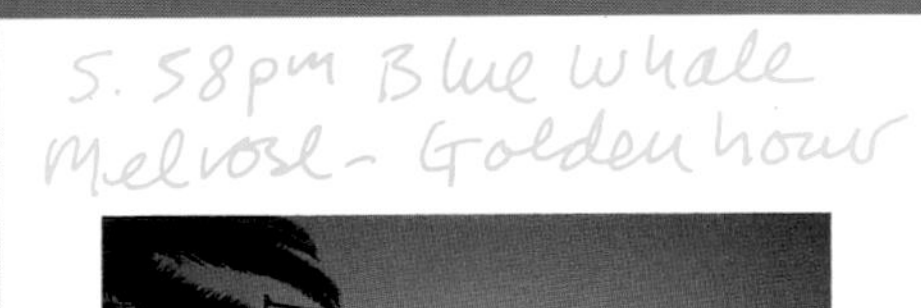

5.58pm Blue Whale Melrose – Golden hour

8:30pm Cadillac Café / West Holly

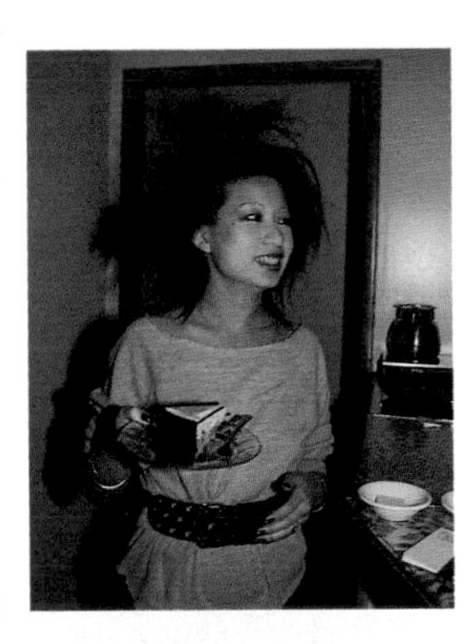

9:00pm Cadillac Café / West Holly

11:10pm West Hollywood / END

MARISSA ROTH

RON KELLEY

Any work day morning at 8 a.m., one can find workers busily creating the "real" dolls that window dresser's dreams are made of.

Right: Cal Trans men work at repairing the streets and freeways damaged by bad weather and bad drivers alike. Where life revolves around the automobile, road work never ends.

Overleaf: An industrial park of perfect symmetry between palm and pavement, provides moments of serenity for the passersby.

RON KELLEY

ANDREJ REISER

TOM VINETZ

KEVIN CLARKE

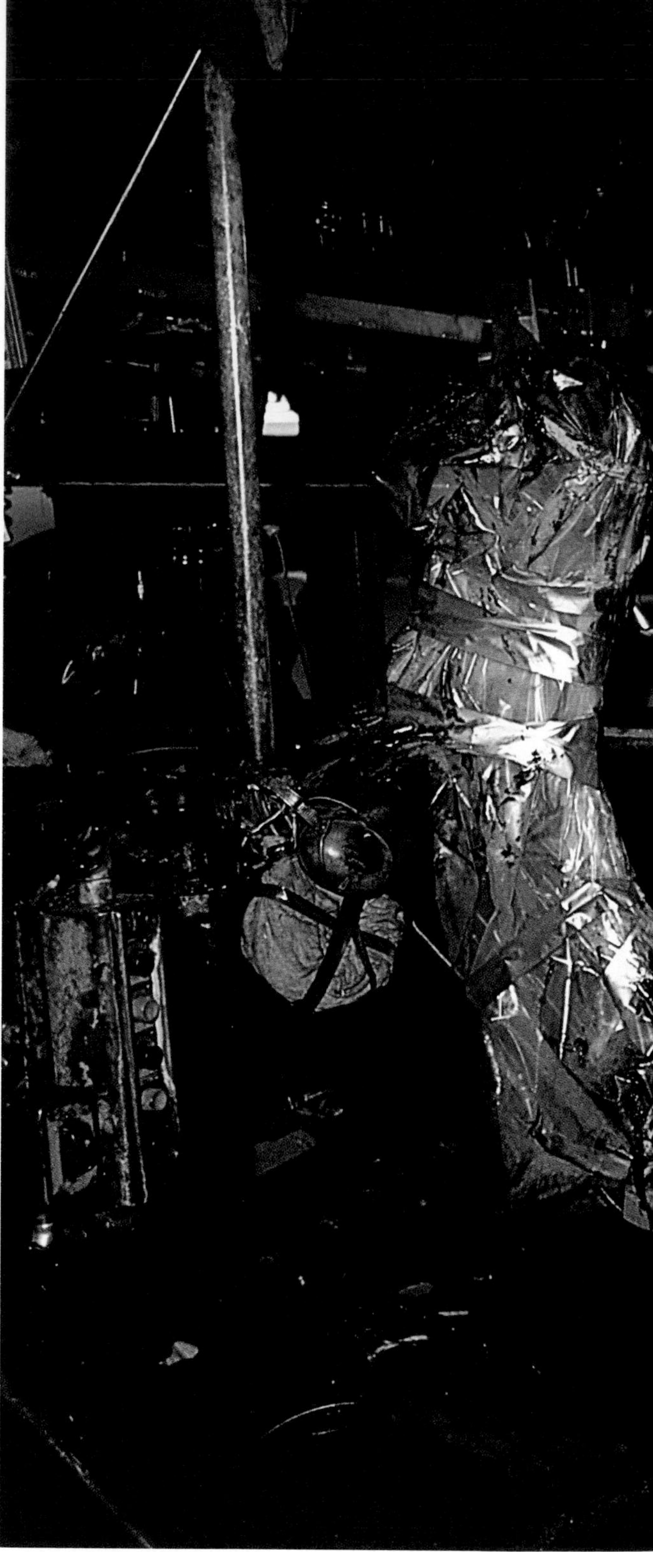

Employees of the *Los Angeles Times* refer to the paper as the velvet coffin because of its great benefits and security. The *Times* is the nation's leader in ad volume, a fact that must delight Don Wright *(left)*, President. The paper has won 13 Pulitzer Prizes over the years.

TOM VINETZ

DENNIS KEELEY/DAN BORRIS

Diana leads Cairo back to the barn at Sunset Ranch.

Left: Diana, Iñacio, Jessie, and Manuel all live at Sunset Ranch, located at the end of Beachwood Canyon, five minutes from the heart of Hollywood. It's 6:30, and Manuel, who is deaf, is waiting for the school bus that picks him up at 7 a.m.

Overleaf: Kids on their way to school at 14 St. and Montana Ave. in Santa Monica. Los Angeles City school buses carry children every day for a trip of up to one hour, 15 minutes.

ANGELES UNIFIED SCH

LINDA WOLF

WILLIAM KLEIN

Waiting for the bus, a schoolboy flashes his student ID in front of a shop on Hollywood Boulevard.

Far right: With the Police looking over her shoulder, Stephanie Greif studies for a Spanish exam in the lounge of the student union at the Westridge School in Pasadena.

NORMAN MAUSKOPF

BOB SEIDEMANN

At 9 a.m. in Long Beach, the United States Air Force accepts delivery of a KC-10A aircraft from McDonnell Douglas. The plane, dubbed "The Extender" by the Air Force, is capable of transporting a maximum load of 170,000 pounds for a distance of 4,370 miles. It takes a year to build each plane. The Air Force has ordered 60 and received 22 thus far.

These two children live in the affluent community of Brentwood. Robby, 8, has started his own collection of large dolls which his parents (who own a similarly impressive collection of Rodin sculptures) hand carried from France. Four-year-old Kate enjoys a lifestyle that is also comfortable.

MARY LLOYD ESTRIN

JACK SHEAR

MITCH EPSTEIN

From Leo Carillo Beach in the north to Laguna Beach in the south, surfers flock to the waves year-round in Los Angeles. Regardless of the break—sand, reef, or point—one factor is constant: territoriality. New faces are not welcome in the water, and fights and vandalism are common during the summer when the crowds become excessive.

Overleaf: Turning everyday sights into visible delights is part of the magic of photography. This bird enjoys his morning bath in the fountain of the Wells Fargo Bank Building in downtown.

BARRY LEWIS

FRANK GARGANI

Artist Mark Gash in his studio near Little Tokyo. Gash has been painting seriously for four years: "I try to paint every day. I get up in the morning and start work. Generally I do people, but lately I've also done some abstract stuff and flowers. I like really vibrant bright colors—almost straight from the tube. Why do I paint? There's nothing else to do."

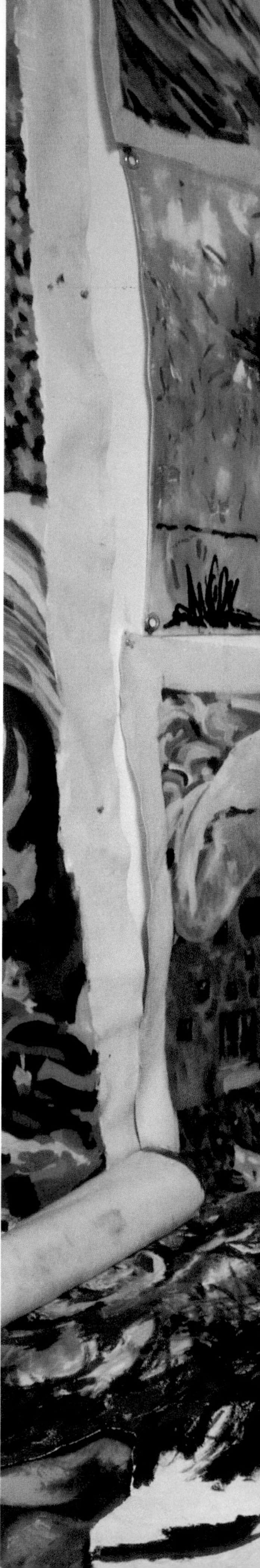

I USED TO DREA
DREAMS OF T
AMERICA T
WHITE FOL
SHOULD BE
I USED
RADIC
OF BLOWING E
AWAY WITH M
POWERS OF C
ANALYSIS, I
TO THINK
ONE TO STO
AND NEGOT
PEACE TH
AND DUG
DREAMED
DREAMS O
A NATURAL
DOING WHA
WOMAN D
SHES NA
HAVE A R

A MILITANT
KEING OVER
SHOW THESE
S HOW IT
DONE,
DREAM
DREAMS
ERYONE
PERCEPTIVE
RRECT
EVEN USED
D BE THE
THE RIOT
TE THE
N I AWOKE
HAT IF I
NATURAL
BEING
WOMAN
T A
DES WHEN
URAL I WOULD
VOLUTION
*(by NIKKI GIOVANNI)
by RAYMOND WRIGH

TOM VINETZ

SYD SHELTON

ERNESTO BAZAN

Morning brings an agonizing wait at the County Department of Social Services in Whittier.

Left: A Watts mother of 15, her three week-old-son, and her younger brother face the starkness of day on Central Avenue.

Prior page: A poem by Nikki Giovanni keeps community pride and spirits high.

LARRY WILLIAMS

Two plainclothes Los Angeles County marshals.

Right: Despite the presence of houses by Frank Lloyd Wright, Richard Neutra, and R.M. Schindler, Los Angeles has a reputation for lacking a consistent architectural style. Natives know otherwise.

Overleaf: A waiter catches up on his reading at a West Los Angeles restaurant.

KENNETH McGOWAN

TOBY GLANVILLE

KENNETH McGOWAN

ARTHUR TRESS

PETER LAVERY

JOHN LONDEI

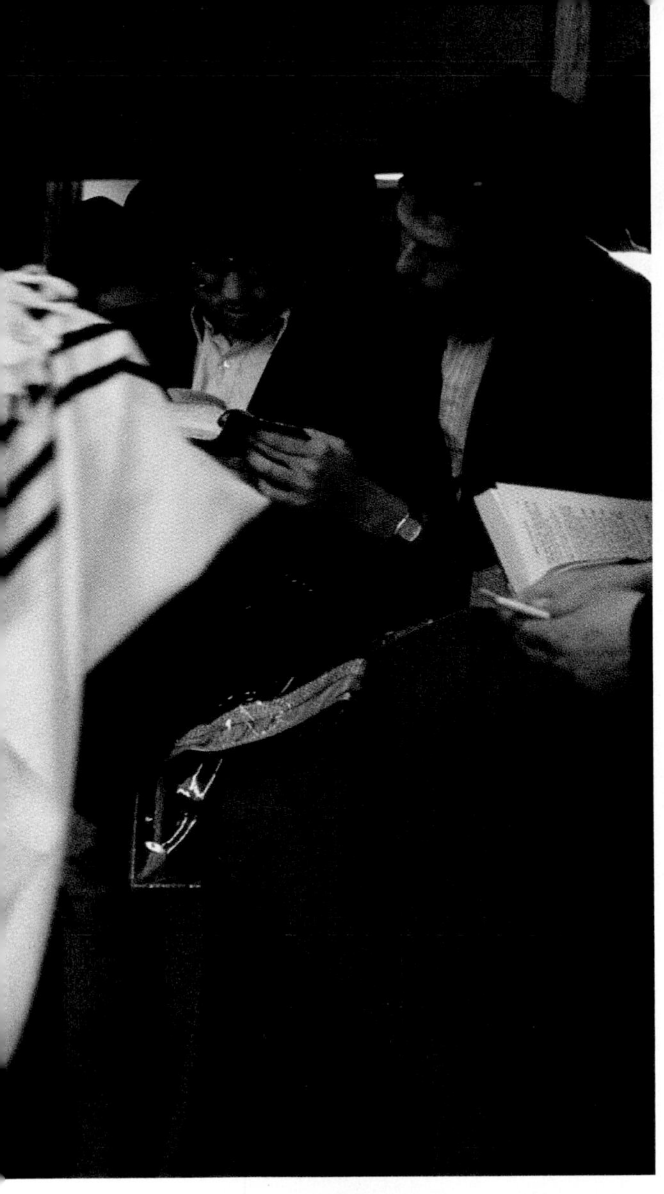

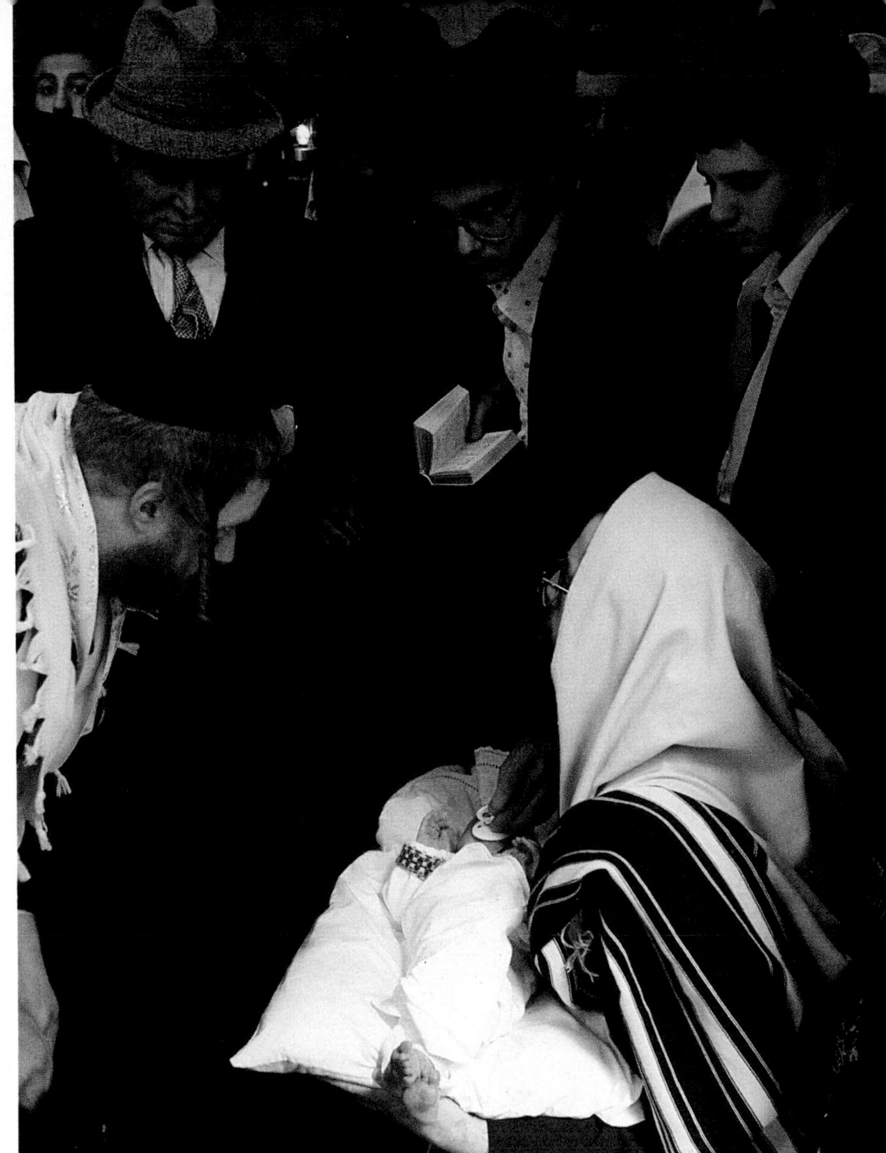

BILL ARON

At the Lubovitch School in the Fairfax district, elders perform a *brit milah* (circumcision), the rite decreed for all Jewish males on the eighth day after birth. Only 55 percent of Los Angeles' half-million Jews are affiliated with any synagogue, orthodox or reform.

Prior page: "Now we have a beach party. Naked girls will do the swim. You shouldn't have been so mean to us. 'Cause now you can't get in. Now we scream "Locals only! Locals only!" ("Locals Only!" by the Surf Punks)

PATRICK BRUCHET

BERNARD FALLON

On an average day, over 11,000 tons of garbage are deposited at the La Puente County Dump, the county's largest public landfill. Roofers Marcus Burnes and Matt Marshall just managed to shovel out a load of rotten shingles before the dump closed.

Prior page: Actress Mae Clarke is often remembered as having a grapefruit pushed into her face by James Cagney in the film *Public Enemy.*

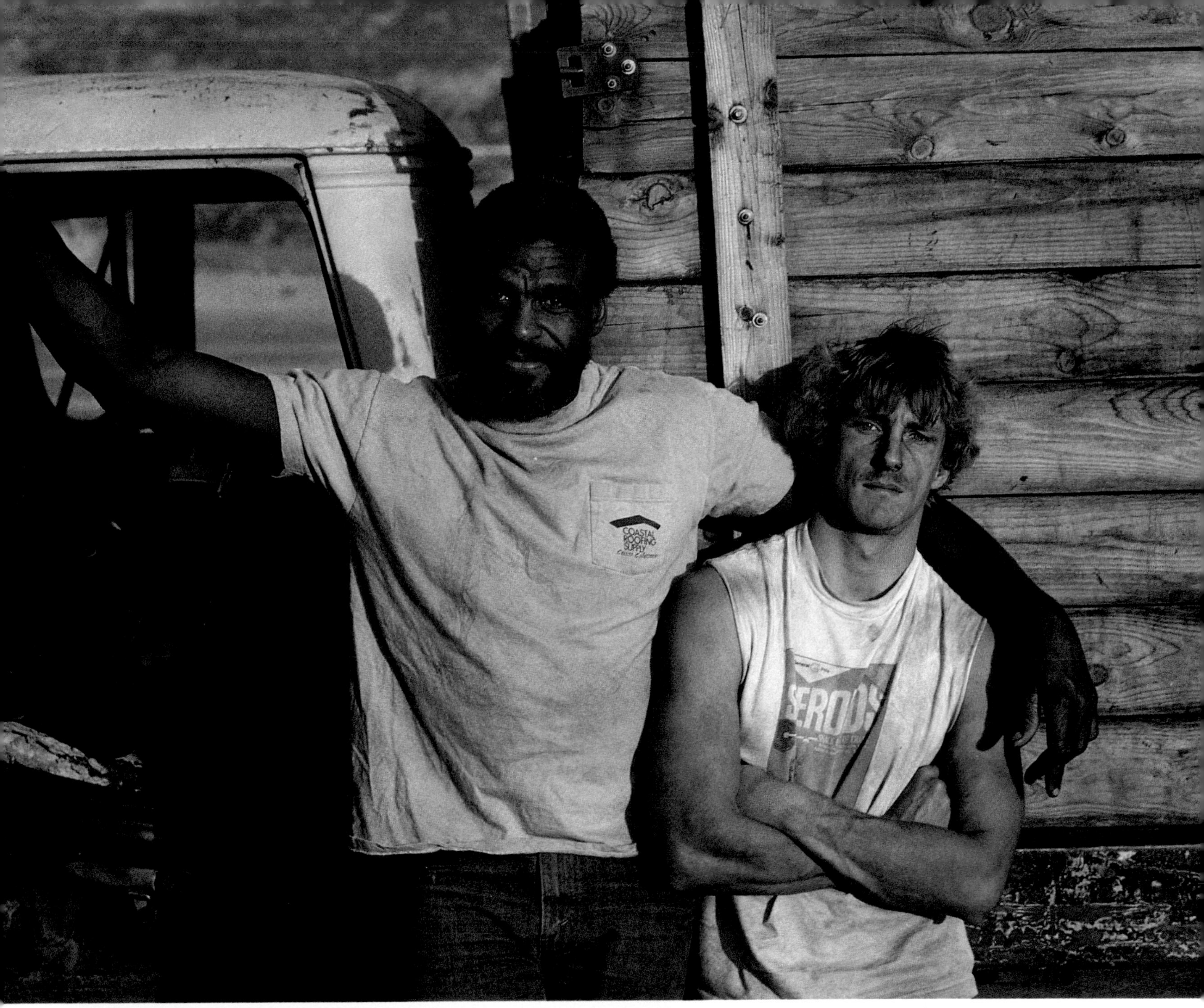
COASTAL ROOFING SUPPLY

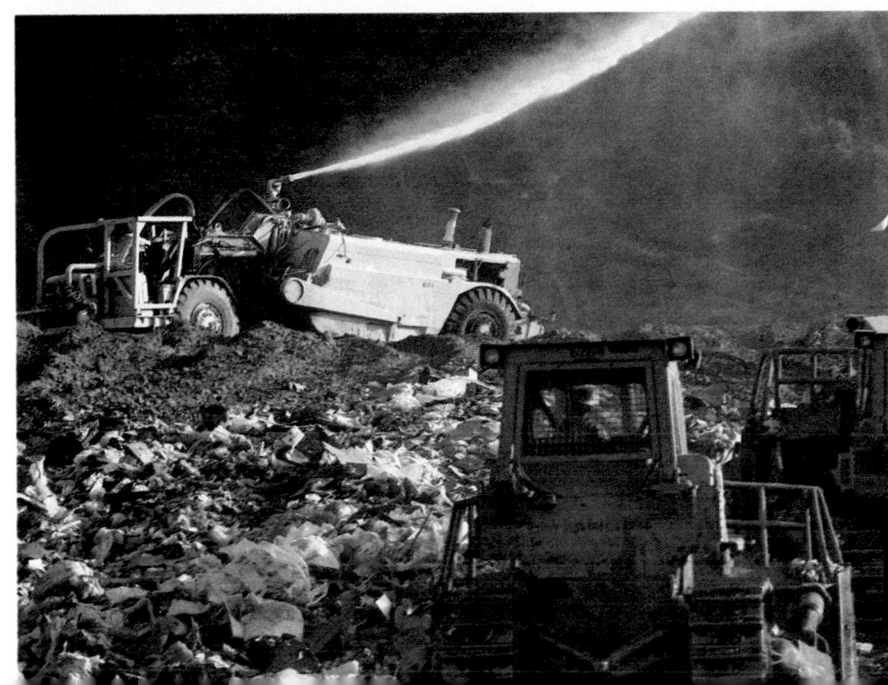

The 25-meter pool at the Sunset Canyon Recreation Center of the University of California, Los Angeles. The outdoor pool is one of six on the campus and is open to all staff, students, faculty, and their families. Over the years, UCLA has contributed repeatedly to the Olympics: 21 male swimmers and divers, 18 female swimmers and divers, and 37 water polo players.

JERRY GORDON

RED SAUNDERS

TIM STREET-PORTER

A residence in the Mount Olympus area of the Hollywood Hills where all the streets are named after Greek gods.

Left: The executive committee members of the Assistance League of Southern California meet to discuss their philanthropic efforts. Over 1,500 women (and a few men) belong to the League.

Overleaf: March in Los Angeles means shirtsleeves and sunshine.

MITCH EPSTEIN

BROADWAY
Vodka is pronounced
Kăm-chat'ka
In the best places.
HARTFORD
ROCKS
MANAGEMENT
223-3325
Vine
466-5101
SPECIAL
WEEKLY RATES
ALLSTAT
ENT-A-CAR
MOLLY'S
PARKING
THEATRE
PARKING
3.00
PAY MACHINE
Coca-Cola
Selma Av

Jet Propulsion Laboratory workers with their Galileo spacecraft.

Right: A mechanic works on wiring of a McDonnell Douglas MD-80 aircraft in Long Beach.

Overleaf: Aerial view of Golfland, a miniature golf course in South El Monte.

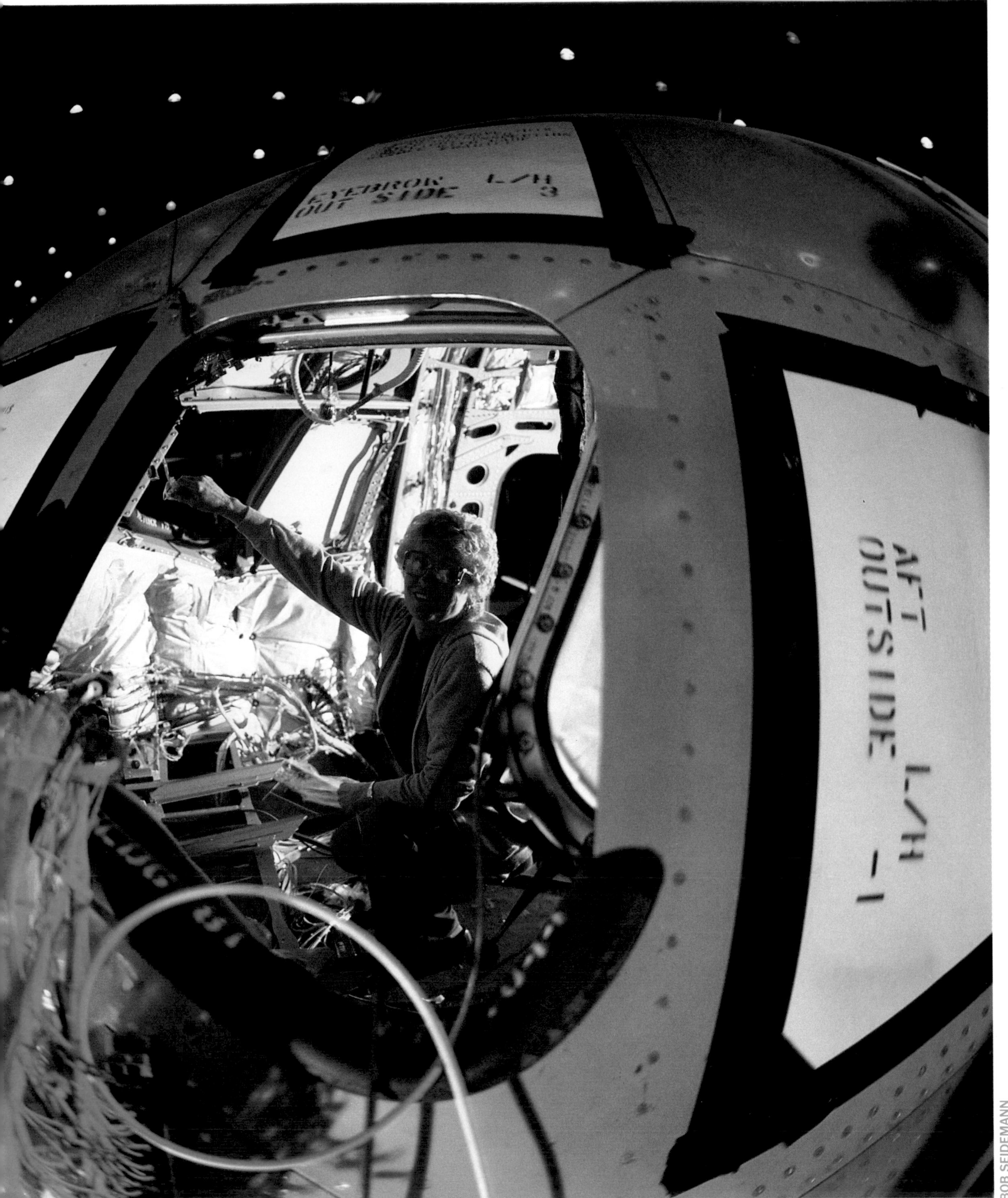

BOB SEIDEMANN

BARRIE ROKEACH

The owner of this North Hollywood gas station says the truck draws customers.

Far right: Employees of the Long Beach Oil Development Company work on a rig at the Long Beach Harbor field. The field, one of the largest in the West, has been producing for 35 years. The current output is 100,000 barrels a day.

Overleaf: Eddie "Animal" Lopez and Randy "Tex" Cobb take a break from sparring at the Main Street Gym in downtown. Owner of the gym is former schoolteacher Carol Steindler, who took over the facility after her father's murder in 1976. "I took on the job to find his killer," she says.

ROMAN LEZO

MIKE ABRAHAMS

BARRY LEWIS

HENRY DILTZ

It's not a Chelsea morning, but a Malibu afternoon, and songwriter-singer Joni Mitchell relaxes to the special music created by waves lapping against the shore.

Right: In the early morning light of his Santa Monica Canyon studio, painter Don Bachardy captures the likeness of playwright-novelist Christopher Isherwood.

JACK SHEAR

GERED MANKOWITZ

P.L. DI CORCIA

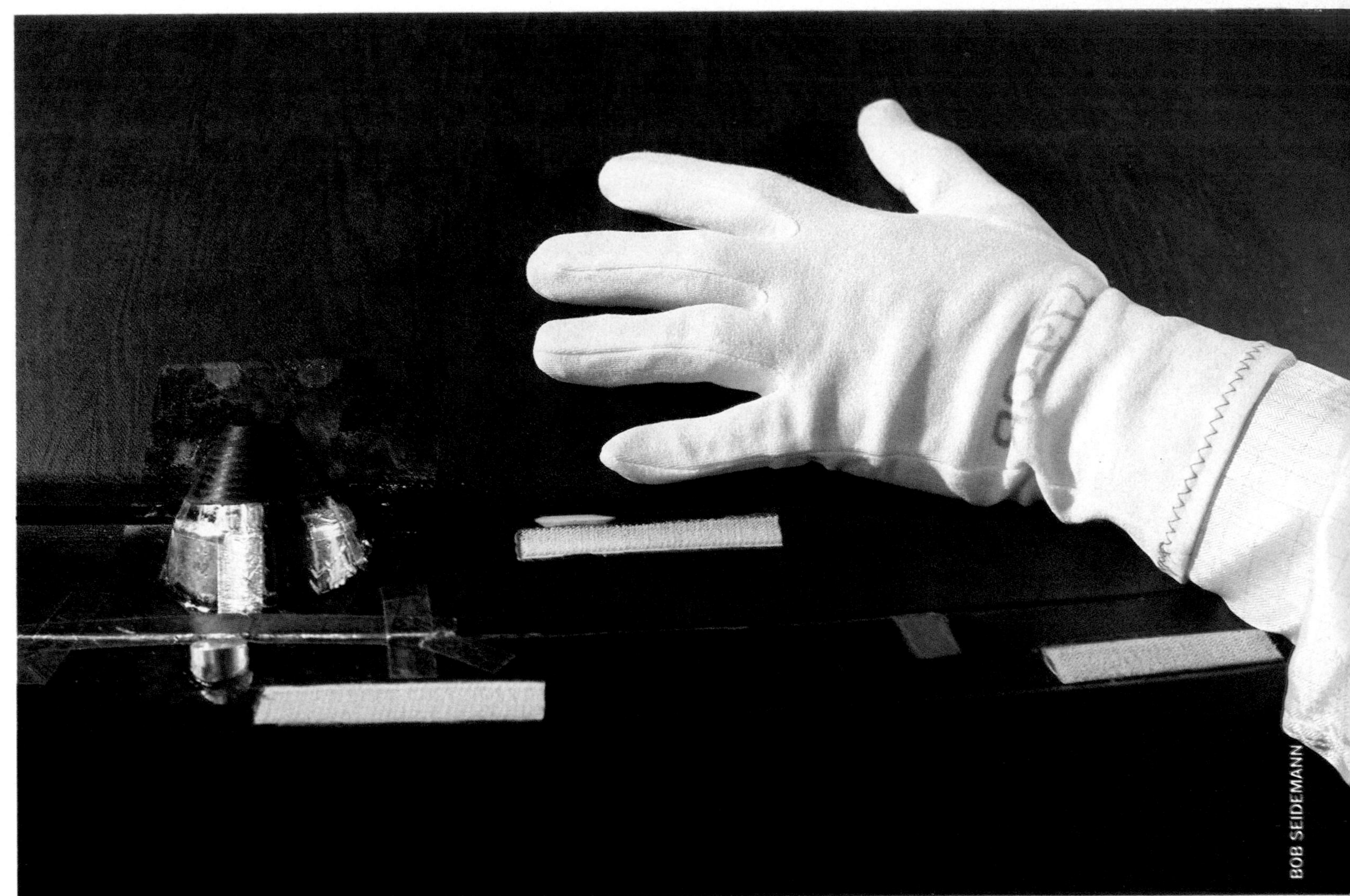

Above: The $110 million Galileo space probe is part of a 5,622-pound spacecraft built by Pasadena's Jet Propulsion Laboratory. In 1986, the probe will go into Jupiter's atmosphere for a historic one-hour data gathering mission.

Left: While anti-nuke protesters wave at cars along Santa Monica Boulevard, a MX missile is launched from Vandenberg Air Force Base. This recent addition to America's arsenal hit its target 4,000 miles away in ten minutes.

RENATE VON FORSTER

CURT JOHNSON

After a month-long trial in Torrance Superior Court, Donna Jelenic is found guilty of first-degree murder in the 1983 stabbing of her husband.

Prior Page: At the Pet Haven Cemetery and Crematory in Gardena, a deluxe dog burial can cost $485. Says a worker, "We bury anything that people have as pets: Snakes, horses, goats, almost anything."

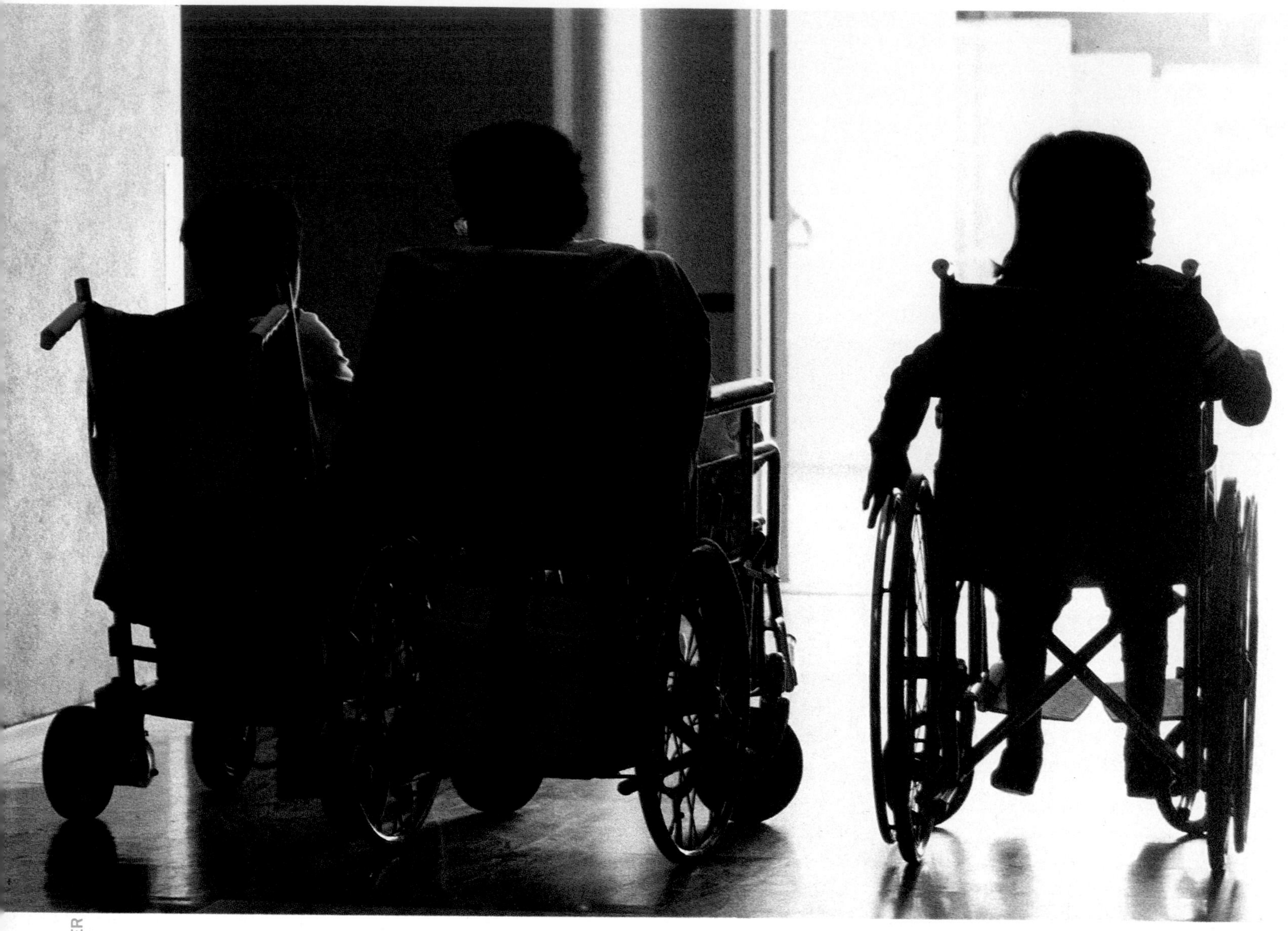

RENATE VON FORSTER

A relaxed morning begins for these handicapped schoolchildren. Many of Los Angeles' schools now provide easy on and off ramps for these students.

Right: A student kicks off her shoes for better (ahem) concentration on her studies.

Far right: At a Beverly Hills nursery school, international performers, Carol Baker and David Carter .

Overleaf: Elysium Fields, a Topanga resort and meditation center, where clothes are optional.

NORMAN MAUSKOPF

LORETTA AYEROFF

ELISA LEONELLI

PETER MARTENS

Crime was down in Los Angeles in 1983, but the 7,000 members of the Los Angeles Police Department were still busy. Although there were fewer rapes, homicides, robberies, aggravated assaults, and thefts, police-related shootings were up with 25 fatalities and 41 woundings. No officers were killed (although six were wounded), but the city is still not considered safe for cops. "I don't know any city that is," commented one LAPD officer, "It's the nature of the job."

PETER MARTENS

ARTHUR TRESS

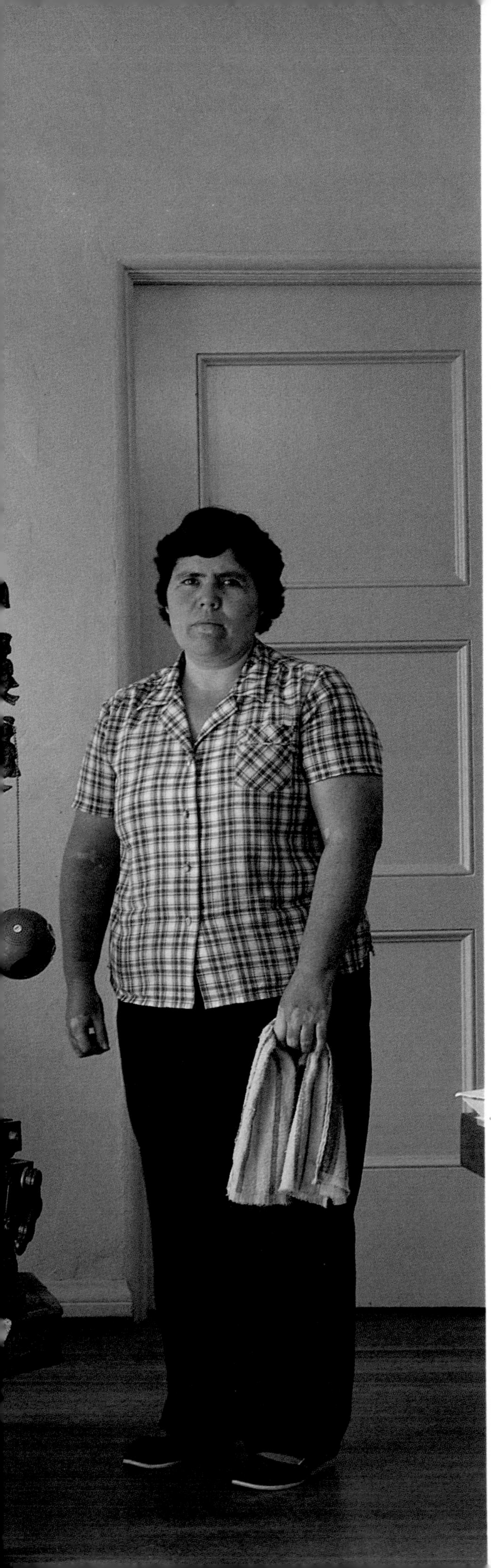

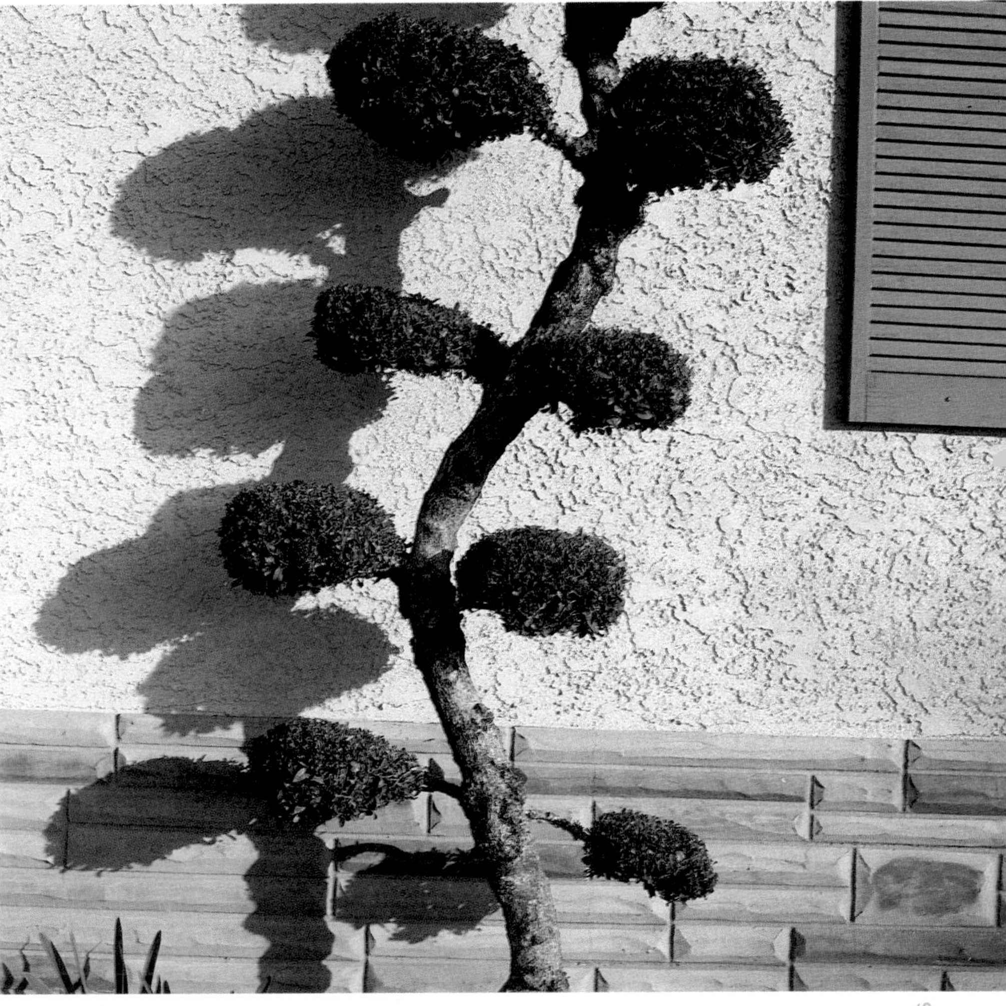

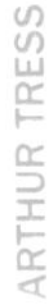

Shrub sculptures in Los Angeles often have a distinctly Japanese cast.

ARTHUR TRESS

Left: Buddha meets Cukor for *Dinner at Eight.* He-Who-Loves-The-Company-of-Women is the name of this Krishna-cum-John Barrymore altar. The film great's Pacific Palisades home now belongs to a professor of Oriental philosophy and art.

GERED MANKOWITZ

STEVE SHAPIRO

Writer-director-producer-actor Mel Brooks shows off a prop from his latest film, *To Be or Not to Be.*

Above right: Larry Hagman, aka J.R. of *Dallas,* welcomes the Olympics to Los Angeles from the roof of his Malibu home.

ROBERT LANDAU

STEPHANE DUROY

LISA POWERS

RAUL VEGA

AVE PILDAS

BASIA KENTON

MIKE ABRAHAMS

RENATE von FORSTER

TED TAMADA

Los Angeles is a city of incongruous images for some, while for a surfer riding a wave, continuity is the name of the game.

BARRIE ROKEACH

BARRY LEWIS

KEVIN LYNCH

SYD SHELTON

TOM VINETZ

On the J-O-B: Far left, a "Happy Birthday" bouquet from his employers is received by a doorman at the Bonaventure. Left, a chauffeur delivers a patron to Chasen's. Above, it's auto wrecking time at a Sun Valley scrap yard. Right, Bunker Hill construction is underway downtown.

VAL WILMER

VAL WILMER

STEPHANE DuROY

ROBERT LANDAU

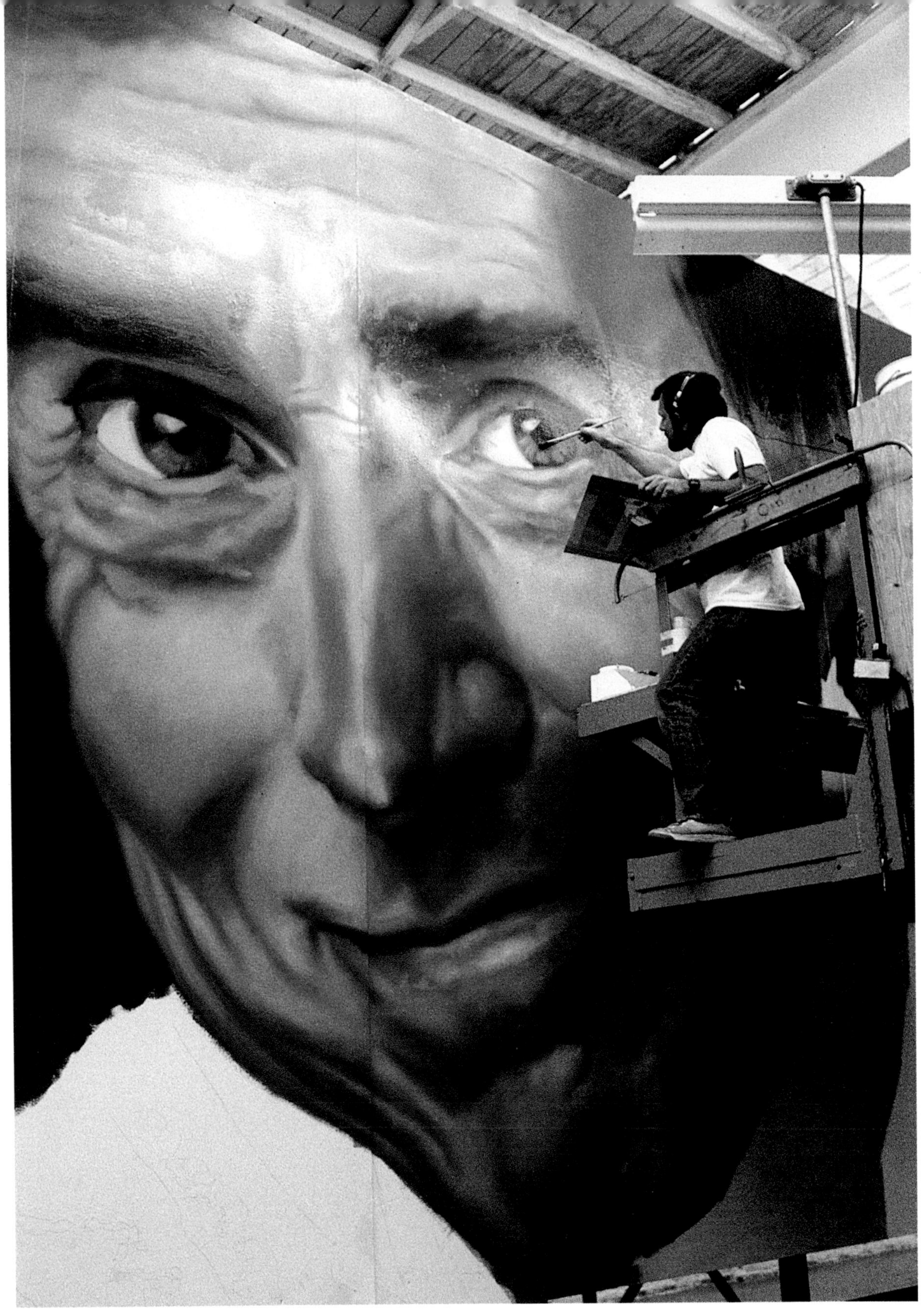

In Los Angeles, billboards are more than just another form of advertising, hyping everything from the latest movies to the hottest rock bands.

Prior page: Legendary blues artists Eddie "Cleanhead" Vinson and Pee Wee Crayton.

ROBERT LANDAU

David Hockney
"Car Parked on Mulholland Drive, March 30, 1984"

Following page: It's sunup in Surf City, U.S.A., made famous by the Beach Boys. Surfing, a craze of the 50s and 60s, has become an established institution.

DAVID HOCKNEY

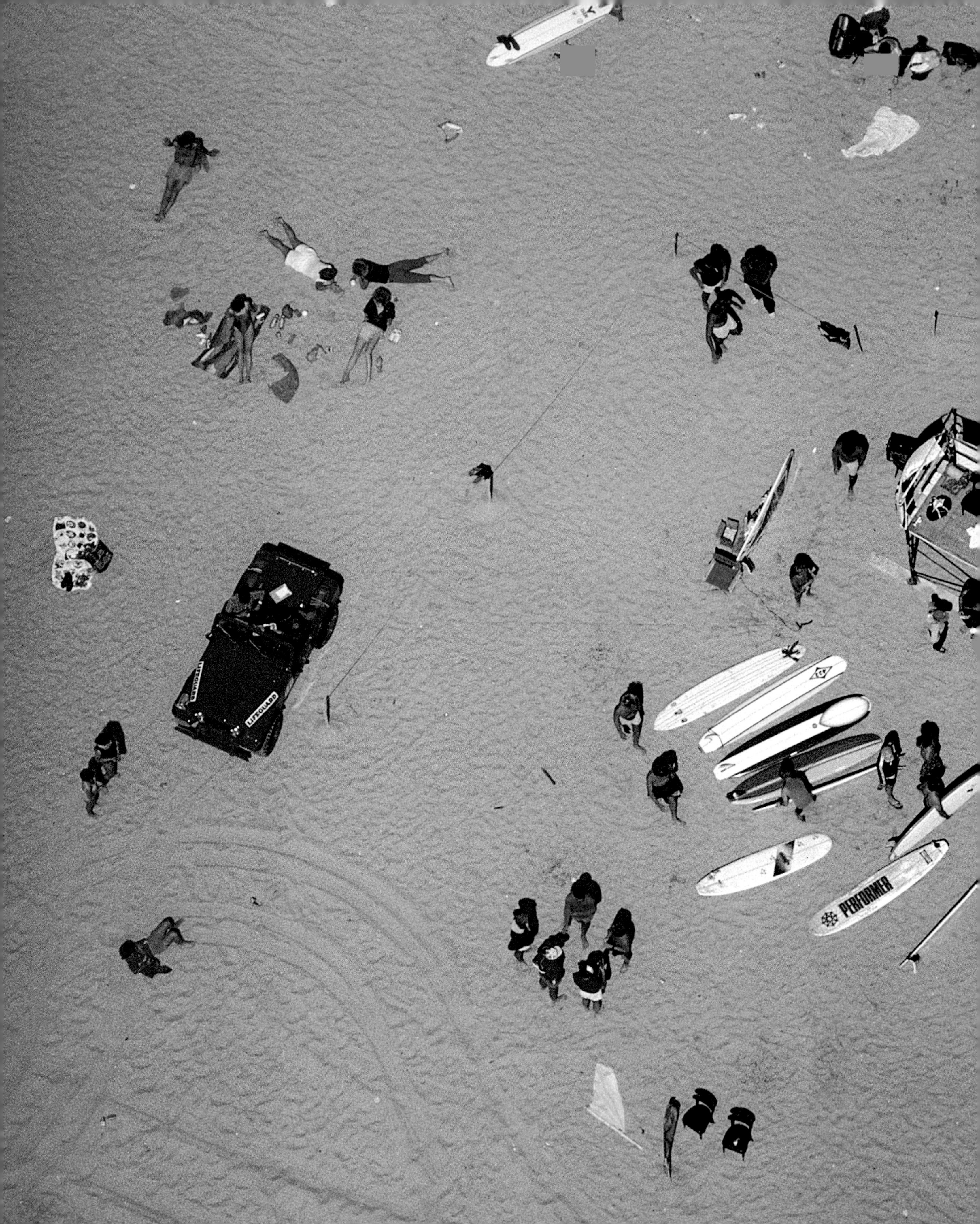
LIFEGUARD
PERFORMER

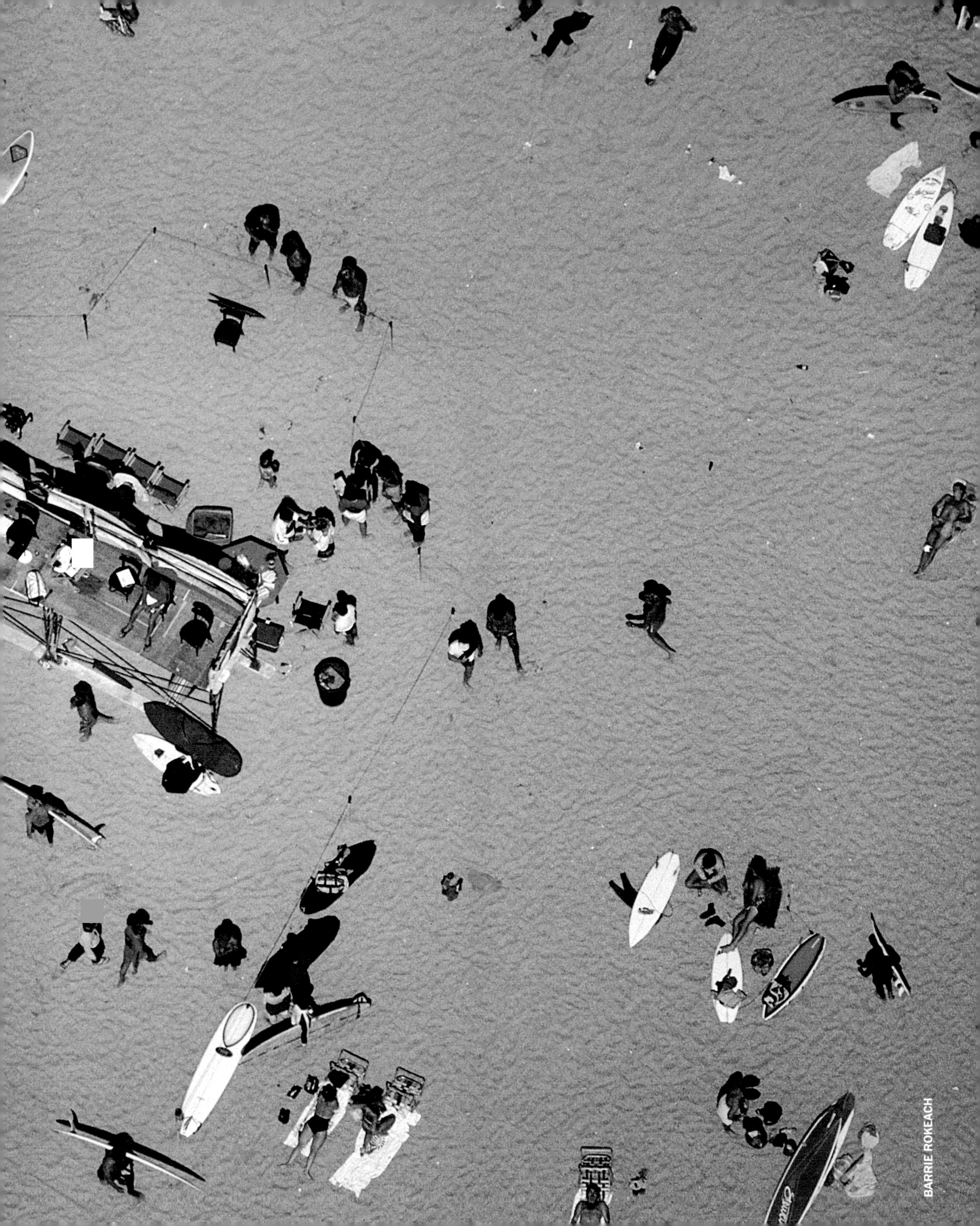

BARRIE ROKEACH

KAREN FILTER

KAREN FILTER

Mamie Van Doren, typed as a sex symbol in the 50s, had just cut a punk record, *Turmoil*. Next to her is true punk Lee Ving of the band Fear, at the Balboa Bay Club in Newport Beach.

Left: Members of the Blasters with blues great Big Joe Turner in his yard in Watts. For the occasion, Blaster Phil Alvin recalls Turner's song, *Central Avenue Blues:* "I'm in the land of sunshine, standing on Central Avenue. I was doin' all right till I fell in love with you. Let's have one more drink baby, and say goodbye to me and you."

MITCH EPSTEIN

Young love blossoms as do poems and songs in the springtime promise of an endless summer just weeks ahead. While the rest of the city toils, dreamers and lovers find better things to do under the warm California sun. They go to the beach, the favorite pastime of Angelenos and the most economical, costing only gas money and the patience to find a free parking place. At beachside Palisades Park in Santa Monica, one can discover the endless summer of one's dreams. The sun and sand, the smog-free air, the palms and tropical trees reaching heavenward; all the makings of a wonderful setting—*la costa*. It is not unusual to find joggers out in the early morning, the elderly taking languid strolls, and bicyclers combining pleasure and exercise in one of the oldest and best kept parks in the area. Nearby property is much higher than in the inner city, as many hunger to share the dream of a home near the blue Pacific. Named for the steep cliffs that line the ocean near by, Palisades Park is considered one of the best places to watch the sunset.

GUGLIELMO GALVIN

REID MILES

"Design is everything," says photographer Reid Miles who composes his set-ups in a style similar to a movie director. His specialty, like that of illustrator Norman Rockwell, is American nostalgia.

Left: At Aquaphoto Products in Hollywood, salesman Sam Parker will go to any lengths (or depths) to demonstrate the company's underwater photo equipment for a customer.

"Los Angeles goes its own blissful, contrary, but well-founded way with food," says Lois Dwan, restaurant critic for the *Los Angeles Times*. "We call it Los Angeles contemporary."

Prior page left: Artist David Hockney in the TV room of his house.

Prior page right: Abraham Nairn, "the next Republican president of America," in Pershing Square.

CHRISTINE HANSCOMB

CHRISTINE HANSCOMB

P.L. DiCORCIA

These people are performing the ritual of Waiting-for-the-Bus. And waiting, and waiting. Only the poor, the "auto" phobic, the young, and the desperate dare ride the bus. Frozen yogurt and falafel shops flourish as shoppers and tired workers mull over humanity's plight or baseball scores. At Los Angeles bus stops, some find religion.

Overleaf: Curandera Doña Anauj performs a white magic ritual cleansing of the body by candlelight in East Los Angeles.

DOUGLAS HILL

GUSMANO CESARETTI

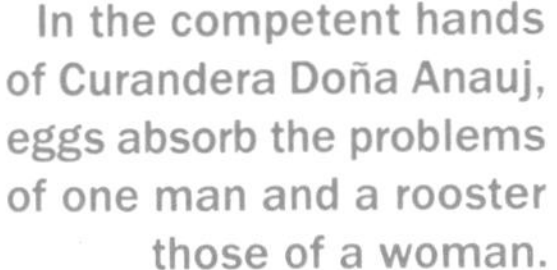

In the competent hands of Curandera Doña Anauj, eggs absorb the problems of one man and a rooster those of a woman.

Prior page: Anauj performs a ritual cleansing of the body using rooster blood, candles, and incense.

Overleaf: An executive takes his noontime break.

GUSMANO CESARETTI

ANDREJ REISER

ARTHUR TRESS

A gardener attends to lush foliage in middle class Mar Vista while a lion-tail agave soaks up sun. The greening of Los Angeles suburbia belies the fact that the city is built on a desert.

RON LEIGHTON

PETER MARTENS

Above: Rose Byrnes and Joe Sanceri are two habitues of Santa Monica's World Gym.

Right: A member of the Bella Lewitzky dance troupe takes a breather during a rehearsal for a dance that will premier at the Olympics Arts Festival.

Far right: A student at the Yoga College of India in Beverly Hills does a back bend, mindful perhaps of founder Bikram Choudhury's words: "Your spine is fabulous." Three times the National Yoga Champion of India, Choudbury has been called the Yoga guru to the stars because of his many celebrity pupils. "If you do yoga every day," says Choudhury, "You never have chronic disease."

TODD GRAY

BASIA KENTON

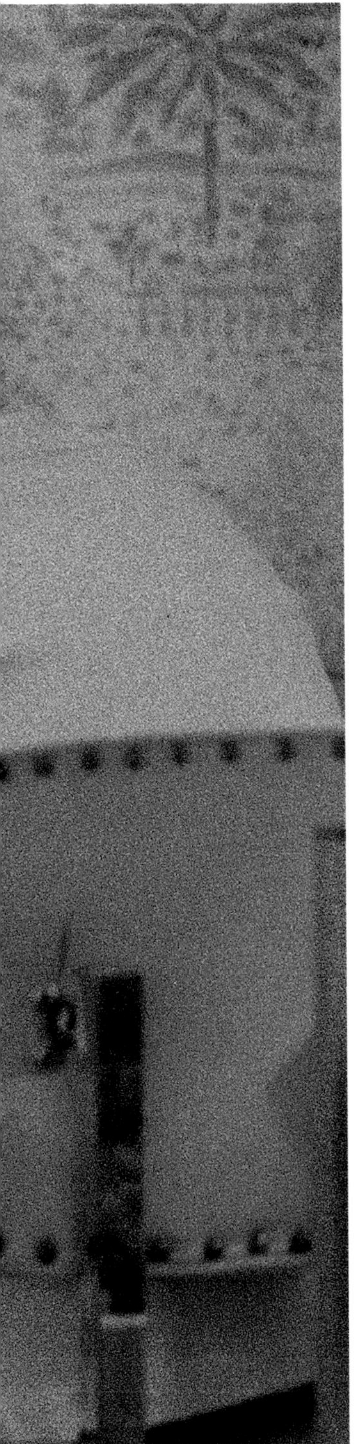

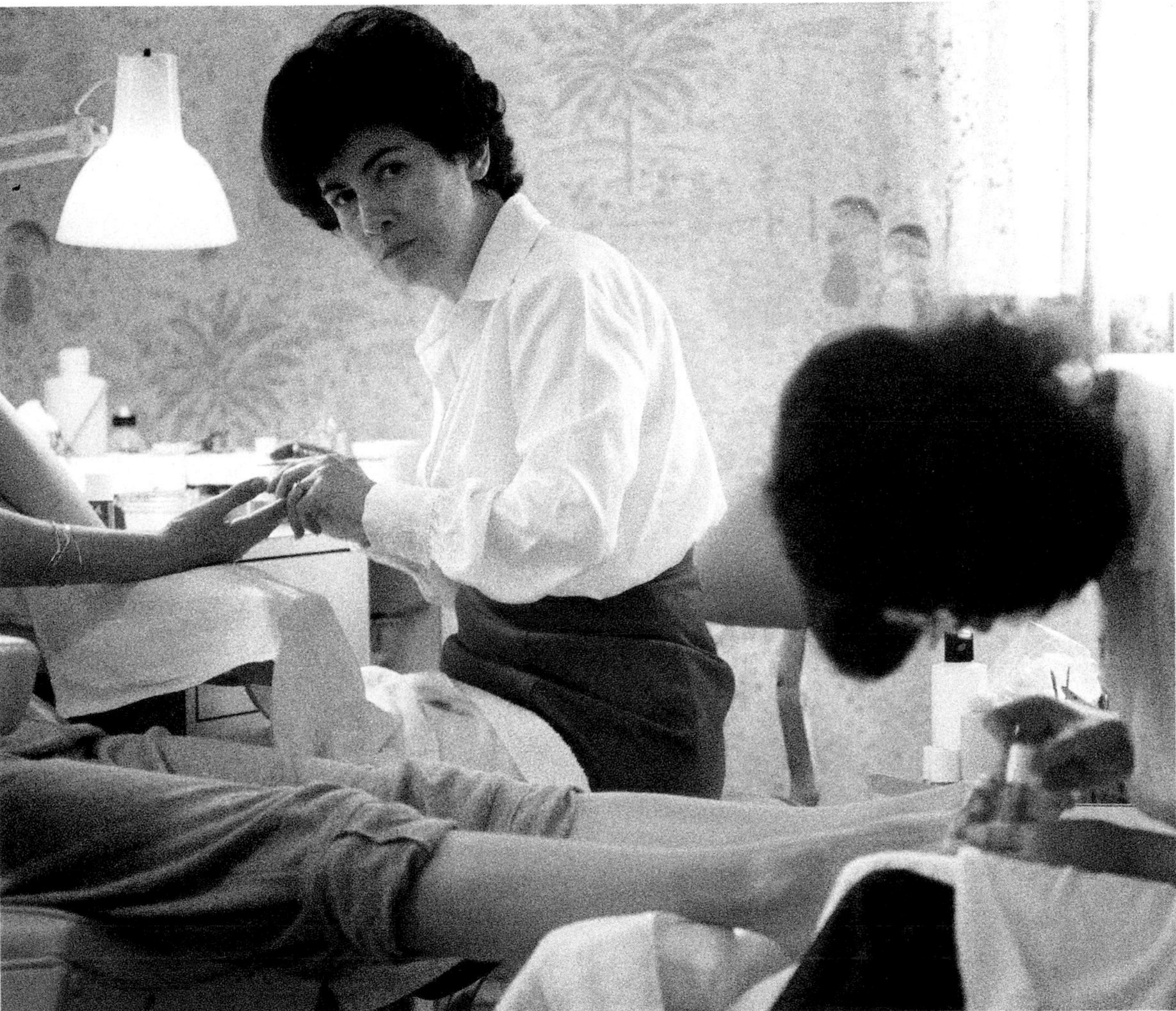

RED SAUNDERS

Image-conscious Los Angeles dotes on lovely nails. Jessica's Nail Clinic, Sunset Plaza, prepares an individual plan after the initial visit.

Overleaf: At their South Broadway clubhouse, you can find The Chosen Few. Los Angeles' best known motorcycle club has ridden together for over 20 years.

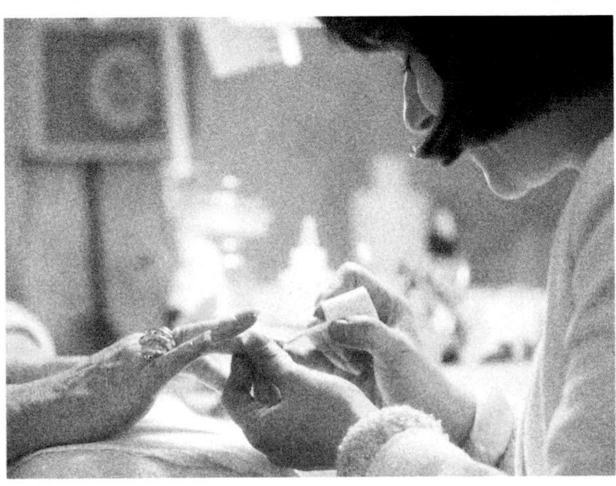

VINCENT MENTZEL

JAMES WOOD

Photographer Wood sets up a 30s. shot in a cyclorama. The resulting picture, above, was used in a self-promotional poster.

Overleaf: Bel Air Patrol General Manager Brian O'Connor (in suit) said, "People go for our service because law enforcement has been reduced, and they feel they have the right to better protection, and they're prepared to pay for it." The Patrol is the oldest and largest (over 100) private police force in Los Angeles. The patrolmen carry Mace, handguns, and batons.

PIERRE TOUTAIN

Tommy's hamburgers are legendary in Los Angeles. The original Tommy's, opened in 1946, has spawned dozens of imitators. The "true" Tommy's, bottom center.

Overleaf: Margaux Mirkin's Drive-a-Dream of Beverly Hills will rent you a helicopter (tuxedoed pilot, cordon bleu meal included) for $550 an hour. Also for rent : dream cars Rolls, or Lamborghini.

VICTOR LANDWEBER

PIERRE TOUTAIN

BASIA KENTON

MARK SHAW

Above: As one of the Pacific Rim's major cities, Los Angeles attracts thousands of Asian immigrants yearly. The result is an exotic blend of cultures and customs. The Kakimoto family are typical. Mr. Kakimoto's ancestry is Japanese; his wife's is Korean.

Right top: A young man meditates at the Self-Realization Fellowship Center in Pacific Palisades while *(right, bottom)* a Korean family enjoys a day in Korea Town.

JAY ULLAL

JOSHUA TOUSTER

Above: Members of the track teams of Venice High School and Pacific Palisades High School limber up before a track meet.

Left: On a closed lifeguard stand at Santa Monica beach, a young woman practices tai chi.

DELLA ROSSA

DELLA ROSSA

Latino youths in Los Angeles *barrios* have developed their own distinctive style. A 1954 Chevy Bel-Air low-rider *(above)* is an essential accessory. Where is this? Look to the young man's hands *(left)* for a clue: EP = Echo Park.

WILLIAM WEGMAN

TIM STREET-PORTER

VOLKER HINZ

VOLKER HINZ

BARRY LEWIS

SHERRY RAYN BARNETT

ROBERT LANDAU

ROMAN LEZO

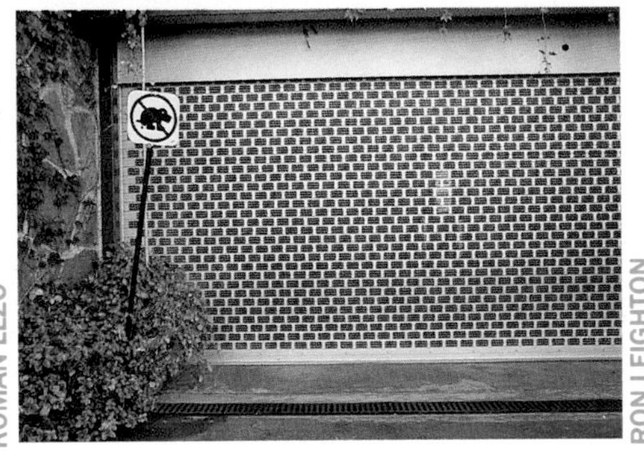

RON LEIGHTON

ELISA LEONELLI

No one can accuse Los Angeles architecture of lapsing into dullness.

Left: Santa Monica's camera obscura offers a panoramic view of city and ocean.

Overleaf: David Hockney "Photographer Missing Reflection in Glass, March 30, 1984".

RENE BURRI

RENE BURRI

RENE BURRI

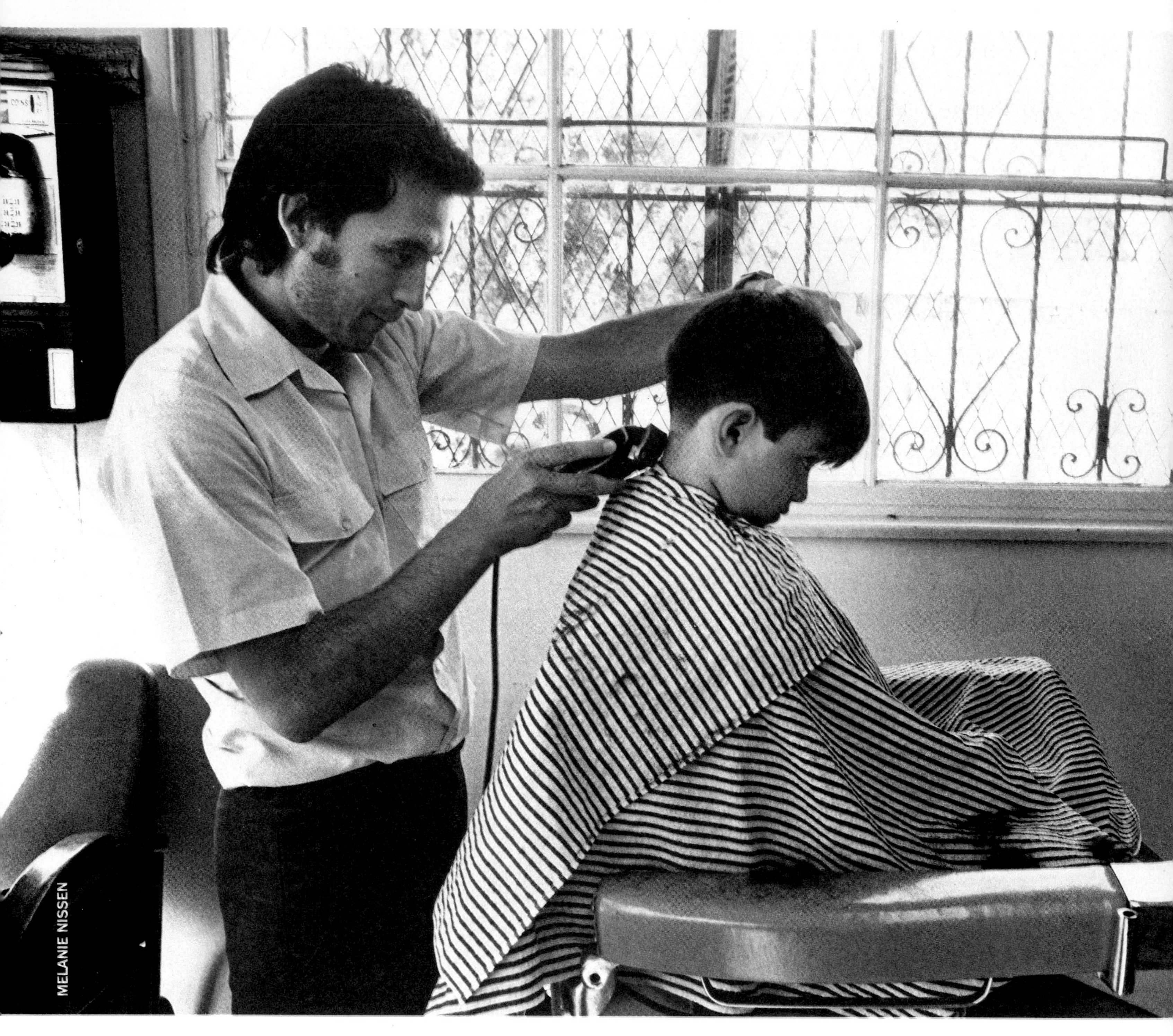

MELANIE NISSEN

VAL WILMER

A couple in Watts.

Left: A young boy gets his hair cut at Armando's Beauty Shop in Pacoima. "It was like a Latino version of a Rockwell," recalls photographer Nissen.

Prior page: While locals do depend on their cars, it's not true that "nobody walks in L.A."

LOYD ZIFF

In health-conscious Los Angeles, jogging is a must as an individual or group fitness activity. Any time of day, and often at night, somewhere in the city, someone jogs.

Right: Prime-time shopping downtown, as at the Broadway Plaza, is a 10 a.m. to dusk affair.

T. TAMADA

MARK SHAW

At the G & W Market in Chinatown, situated directly north of downtown Los Angeles, this worker carries two proud birds to their inevitable destinies as *kung pao* chicken or *moo goo gai pan*. As a culinary delight, few deny that chicken has given the hamburger and the hot dog a run for the money.

Right: Towering over passersby on Broadway is Chicken Boy, a monument to the golden reign of chicken shacks which provide every possible variation on the mouth-watering themes of Southern fried, and finger-lickin' good.

MARI UMEKUBO

WILFRIED BAUER

Walking in Los Angeles is a part-time occupation, hard on the shoes. One does it for exercise, contemplation, to pick up some hastily needed item from the neighborhood store, to browse in shopping malls, to walk one's child to school, or to cross the street after having parked one's automobile on the other side. No one takes walking seriously here.

BERNARD FALLON

Until his father Roberto took him to Torrance's Sharpshooter Indoor Range, 8-year-old Patrick Aparicio had never fired a gun before. He squeezed off six shots and hit the bull's-eye four times.

Right: Range co-owner Joe Gaines and his brother Garth sharpen reflexes on video games.

PAUL MAXON

DENNIS KEELEY / DAN BORRIS

Don Davis and his wife Rae manage an apartment building in Hollywood, but that isn't what has landed him in the Guiness Book of World Records for the last ten years. That fame came as a result of "Totalmedia," Davis' one-man-band act that has him playing more musical instruments at one time than any other human has ever ventured. Although Davis may be amazing, he's not always musical. Wisecracked photographers Keeley and Borris: "Don's one-man band sounds similar to a trainload of pigs colliding with a trainload of car parts."

Prior page: The water-spitting rubber shark on the Universal Studios tour has been a wet hit with tourists for years.

SYD SHELTON

NORMAN MAUSKOPF

This man who learned to bevel glass as a child in Armenia now works in Pasadena.

Right: Each morning, Granny feeds the ducks along a Venice canal.

Prior page: At 4:30 p.m. a soldier mourns the death of a friend in Roosevelt Memorial Park, Gardena.

BASIA KENTON

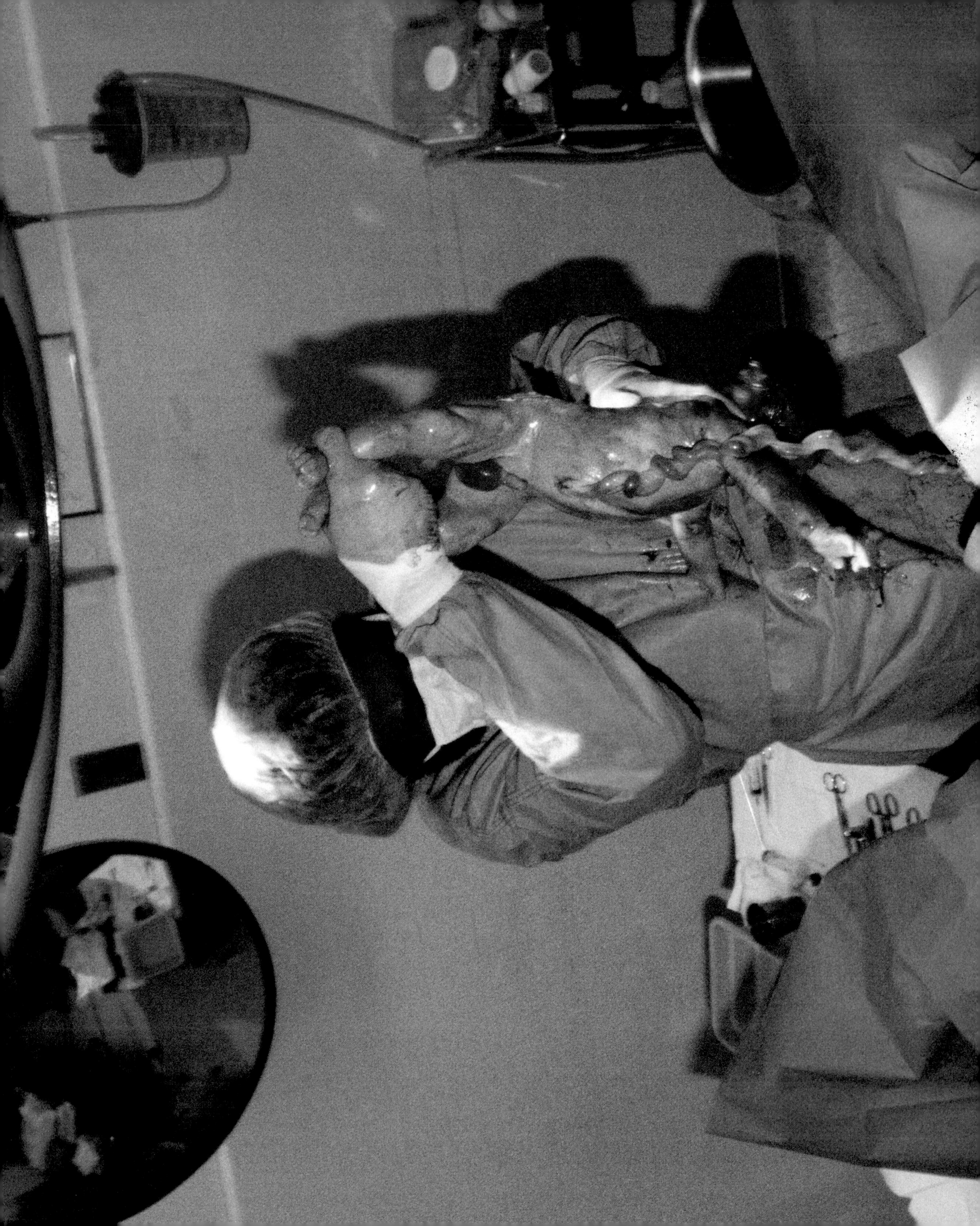

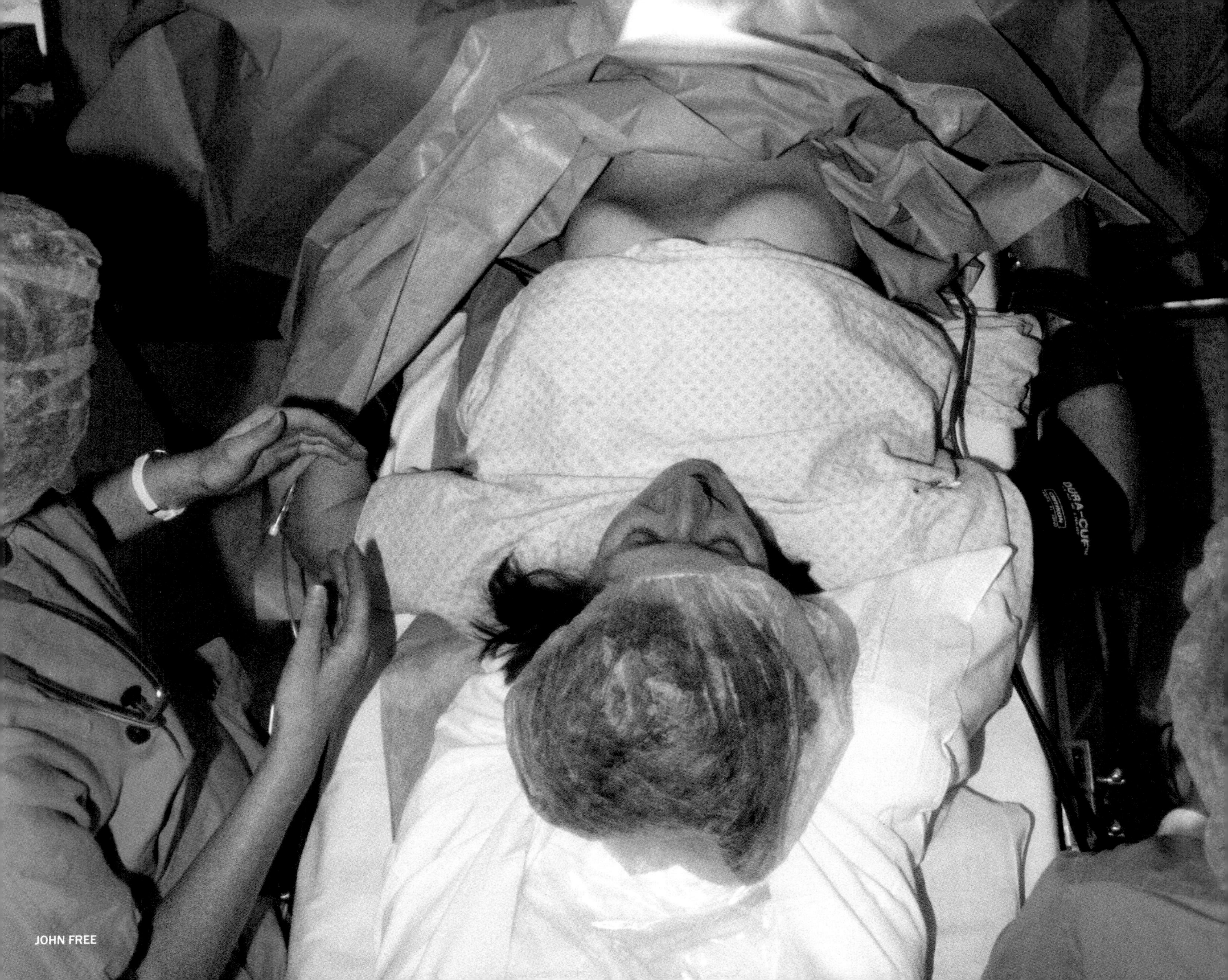

JOHN FREE

PETER REISS

An inmate at Norco's Rehabilitation Center.

Right: Ninety-nine percent of the nearly 400,000 Central American refugees here are undocumented aliens and live daily with the fear of an Immigration raid hanging over their heads. Most make do living in cramped quarters and working for below minimum wage. This group of three families reside in a one-bedroom apartment in downtown.

Prior page: After a twenty-hour labor, Christopher Vasques is delivered.

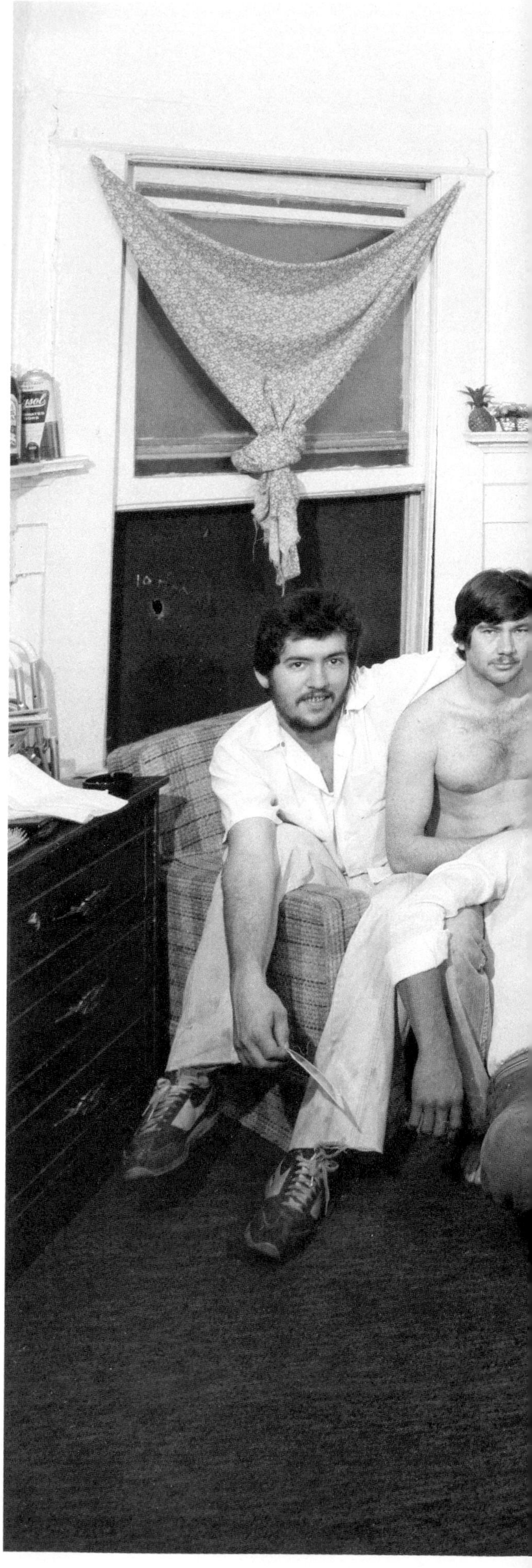

JEFFREY SCALES

WILLIAM MIDDLEBROOK

The line for free meals at the Midnight Mission at 4th and Los Angeles streets in downtown forms hours before the doors open. Some people spend the night on the sidewalk waiting for breakfast. The Midnight Mission, founded in 1914, is known as the Hilton of the missions by local transients because of the quality of food and cleanliness. In a typical day, the mission feeds 1,500 people and provides beds for 138. In the last five years, says a worker, the lines have doubled in size.

ANDREW MOORE

Sylvia's Bail Bonds in San Pedro is open 24 hours a day. Says the proprietor, "The jail is right over there. I'm here because they don't like to go too far."

Left: This interchange of the Golden State Freeway with the Foothill Freeway near Sylmar is the world's tallest. It was also the site of the 1971 Sylmar earthquake, the most devastating local temblor in recent memory. The quake killed 65 people and collapsed large chunks of the freeways.

MELANIE NISSEN

LINDA WOLF

Schoolgirls in Brentwood.

Left: A Cabbage Patch treasure for three Studio City girls.

ERNESTO BAZAN

There isn't much to do on a hot afternoon in the barrios of East Los Angeles, but play. Idleness and rejection from the mainstream has forged a youth gang subculture of Latino lions who have turned their bitterness into battle cries.

Far right: Young break dancers have found a positive alternative.

12

ELSA FLORES

DENNIS CALLWOOD

DENNIS CALLWOOD

A proud father pays a street photographer for the Polaroid print of his beautiful little daughter.

Left: It is *quinceaños.* At Our Lady Queen of Angels Roman Catholic Church, a girl of 15 begins womanhood. She is coming out into society, and this is her debut. Mexican traditions and rituals are very much alive in El Pueblo de Los Angeles Historical State Park. Similarly designed to the plazas of old Mexico, this area is the designated birthplace of Los Angeles.

Prior page: At the South Pasadena-San Marino YMCA, baby swim class teacher Kay MacInness instructs infants and mothers.

MARK HANAUER

It is 7 p.m., one hour before show time. At La Cage Aux Folles on La Cienega Boulevard, this star applies makeup before going on. Is it Joan Collins? Wrong. *He* makes up into a *she* to the cacophony of "girl" talk, the clatter of high heels and dangling beads, beneath a thin veil of cigarette smoke. Female impersonation in Los Angeles dates back to Sir Lady Java.

Far right: Portraits taken at a friend's dinner party reveal prominent men on the local arts scene. *Clockwise, beginning at top left: Dynasty* producer Doug Kramer; hot young painter Ed Ruscha; Pontus Hulten, formerly founding director of the Museum of Contemporary Art; abstract painter Ellsworth Kelly.

ROBERT MAPPELTHORPE

ROBERT LANDAU

Art? Landmark? Pop architecture? Two examples of 30s hard sell that began with the Hollywood sign in 1923.

ROMAN LEZO

TODD GRAY

It is sunrise at Crocker Center in downtown Los Angeles . The tallest building is the First Interstate Power building which is 62 stories high.

Far left: With New Wave and the revival of the 50's, the hamburger is alive and well in the Valley at Carl's Jr., on Ventura Boulevard in Sherman Oaks, and so is the French poodle.

LINDA WOLF

LOU STOUMAN

Left: The shadows of playing children along a wall in Compton.

Above: Many of the homeless sleep in abandoned autos, on bus stop benches, and in the doorways of businesses closed for the night. This woman sleeps in Santa Monica's Palisades Park.

VOLKER HINZ

In the splendid quiet of his richly furnished Hancock Park home, Muhammad Ali kneels to the east on his prayer rug. The three-time boxing heavyweight champion of the world and devotee of Islam has settled at the periphery of the public eye.

JAY ULLAL

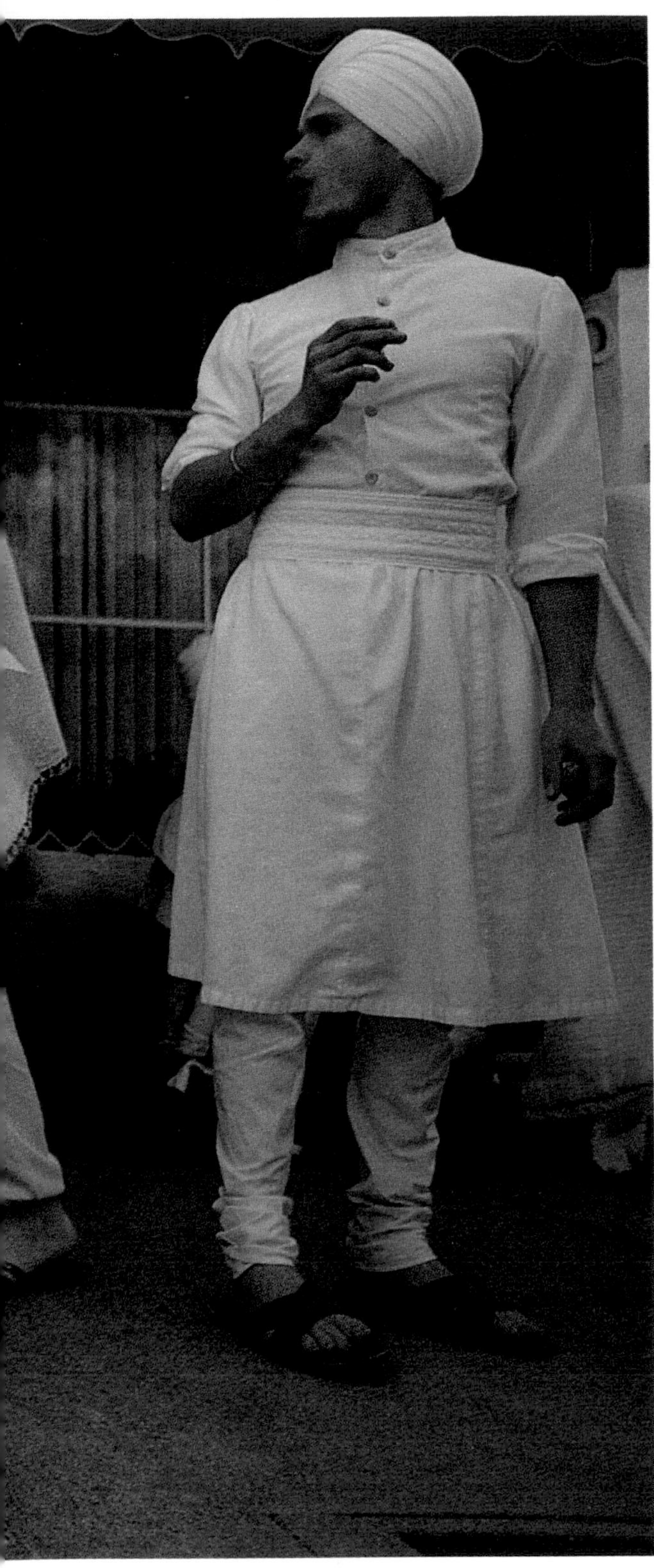

Like New York, Los Angeles is a major urban center for American Sikhs. The religion (which is the sixth largest in the world) eschews the use of tobacco, coffee, alcohol, and meat. The cutting of any body hair is also forbidden. "We have a lifestyle that promotes righteous living and having families" says a Sikh from the Guru Ramdas Ashram in West Los Angeles."It creates a happy, holy life." In the past five years the congregation of the Ashram has more than doubled.

GREG O'LOUGHLIN

Six people started this sand castle on Venice beach at dawn. Twelve hours later, it fell to the waves.

Right and overleaf: The art of photography is not just the domain of adults as these pictures taken by 11 youngsters (aged 6 to 12) prove. The kids used Kodak Disc cameras with auto focus for the job.

Onis Garcia age 11

Onis Garcia age 11

Joshua Castillo age 11

Travis deZonia age 10

Leah Washburn age 9

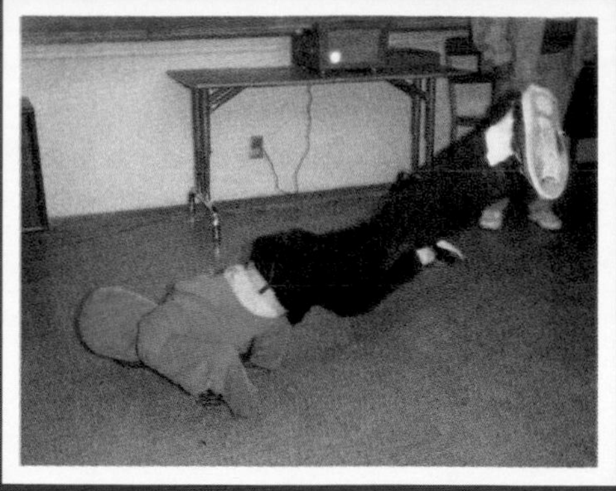
Karl Simon age 12

Travis deZonia age 10

Stephanie Castillo age 7

Paul Londei age 6

Karl Simon age 12

Leah Washburn age 9

Anna Londei age 8

Travis deZonia age 10

Anna Londei age 8

Akosua Brown age 11

Leah Washburn age 9

Philip Castillo age 7

Stephanie Castillo age 7

Philip Castillo age 7

Paul Londei age 6

Iman Hobbs age 9

Onis Garcia age 11

Atiya Hobbs age 8

Anna Londei age 8

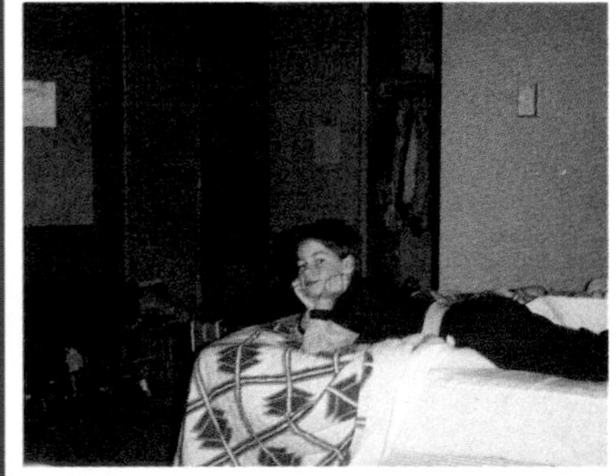

Anna Londei age 8

Onis Garcia age 11

Leah Washburn age 9

Leah Washburn age 9

VOLKER HINZ

VIDEO
RENT
CAR

E.K. WALLER

Hollywood punks routinely ask for money from tourists who ask to take their picture.

Prior page: These 400-foot cylinders of mirrored glass make up the Bonaventure Hotel, a tourist's dream of shops, glass-walled elevators, and restaurants.

For his 24 hours, photographer Paul Fortune Fearon spent the entire day in front of a television, something that some people do quite regularly. The daily national average for television viewing in America is now nearly seven hours according to the Nielsen ratings service. That figure is the highest ever recorded. While the viewership is up, the quality still leaves something to be desired. The most popular show during the *24 Hours* project was *Dallas* which pulled in an 18.1 rating. For a 30-second spot on *Dallas,* CBS charges anywhere from $125,000 to $200,000, depending on the weekly ratings.

San Diego Frwy
ELLFLOWER BLVD.

Hart

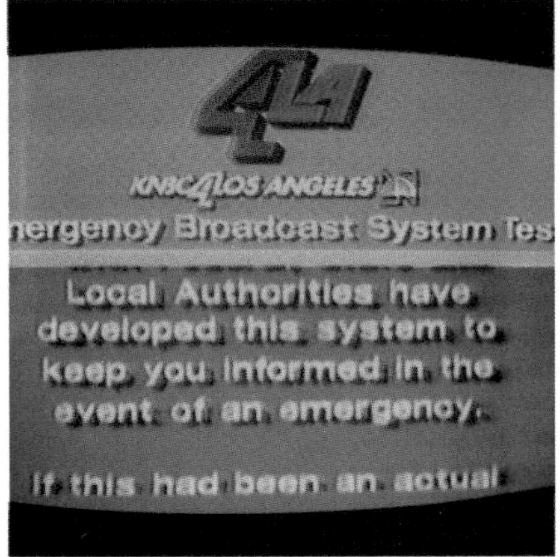
4
KNBC 4 LOS ANGELES
mergency Broadcast System Tes
Local Authorities have developed this system to keep you informed in the event of an emergency.
If this had been an actual

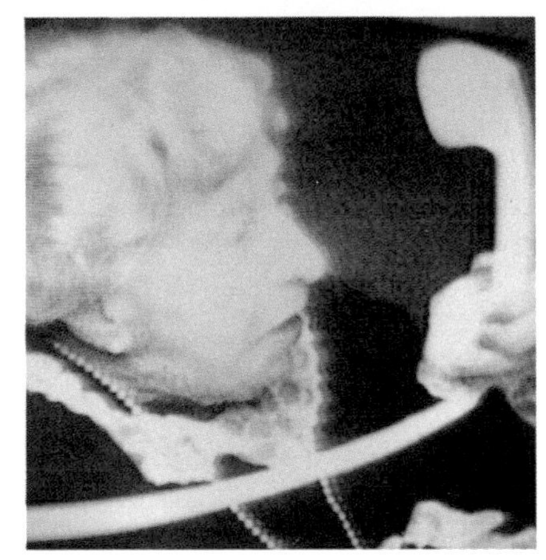

WIFE'S FATHER
BRIDE & GROOM
BRIDE'S PARENTS
SPINS
1

(714) 731-1000
1-800-421-2221

GERED MANKOWITZ

BRITAIN HILL

Writer-actor Buck Henry poses proudly with his personal satellite dish antenna, capable of picking up over 100 television stations.

Left: Actor Charlton Heston, backstage at the Ahmanson Theatre where he was starring in the play, *Detective Story.* The bandage on his hand covers a spider bite.

RENATE von FORSTER

Take a stroll along the insistent pavement where First Street and Lorena join to El Mercado, the market place. They will be there, the mariachi players. Here you can simultaneously shop at leisure and enjoy their romantic rhythms, daring lilts and heady ballads, ancestors of *salsa*. You may find them Friday, Saturday or Sunday from five to midnight, evoking the essence of black soil and sun-brown girls with braids. You may join the players in song, if you desire, but you must pay as is the custom.

STEPHEN F. SOMERSTEIN

In Burbank, host Gene Rayburn starts the *Match Game* and *Hollywood Squares Hour*, a popular afternoon entertainment for students, senior citizens, and professionals.

Right: Master of tai chi chuan, a Chinese martial art, begins his class in Hollywood.

Below: Hare Krishna devotees pray at the International Community of Krishna Consciousness in Culver City.

BASIA KENTON

JAY ULLAL

RED SAUNDERS

GERED MANKOWITZ

Celebrity look a likes are a big business in Los Angeles. While Marilyn Monroe, Michael Jackson and Elvis Presley are perpetual favorites, the most requested face these days is Ronald Reagan.

Right: A look a like of another type, this Bel-Air patrolman has the same powers of arrest as any citizen.

PIERRE TOUTAIN

From the director of "An Officer and A Gentleman"
comes a different kind of film.
A NEW VISIONS PRODUCTION · A TAYLOR HACKFORD FILM
AGAINST ALL ODDS
NOW PLAYING.
RESTAURANT
BREAKFAST
LUNCH
DINNER
Horn Ave
Holloway
3174
968.

VOLKER HINZ

RED SAUNDERS

Making an uneventful trip through cross-town traffic in the late afternoon rush hour from 4 to 6 p.m. is a feat few can accomplish without severe aggravation in the City of Angels. This jam on the Sunset Strip is indicative of the "daymare." Friendly tip: Avoid Fairfax between Sunset and Pico at all costs.

ERNESTO BAZAN

Family celebrations, weddings and birthdays are immortalized at the Anthony Loya Studio & Tuxedos on Whittier Boulevard in East L.A. where brides still blush, grooms beam in pride and even a baseball player is candidly captured.

LOVE YOU
Love

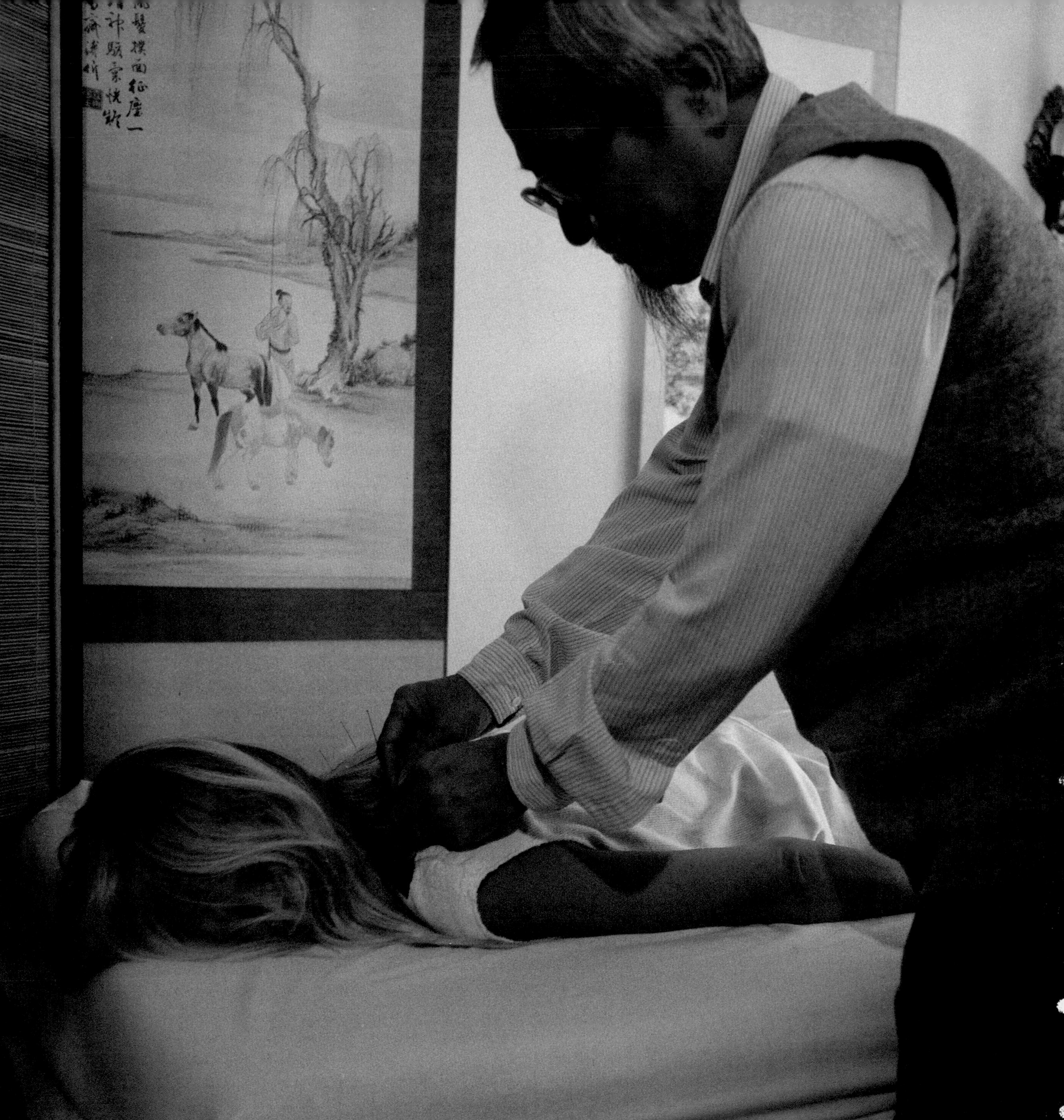

BASIA KENTON

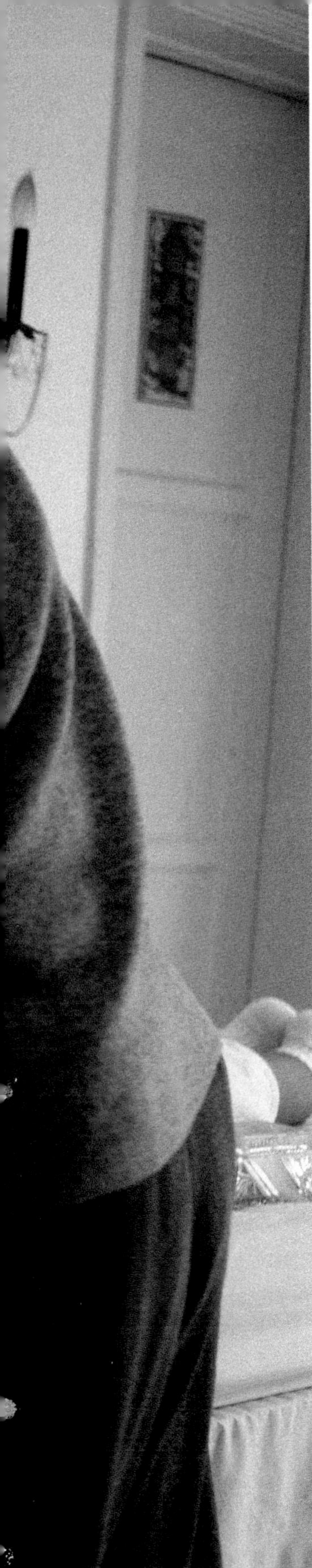

Business is brisk at The Buttery, a Santa Monica bakery.

Left: One of acupuncture's local champions is Taoist master, Ni Hua Ching. At his home amid Brentwood's tree-lined lanes, he reunites spirit, mind, and body of a satisfied patron.

BASIA KENTON

SCOTT BROCK

JOSHUA TOUSTER

At an indoor soccer game at the Inglewood Forum, the Los Angeles Lazers went down to defeat 6 to 5 at the hands of the Baltimore Blasts.

Left: Paula McGee of the University of Southern California goes up for a basket in a semi-final championship game against Louisiana Tech. USC won, 72-67.

There are over 6 million cars in Los Angeles County, a fact that delights both salesmen (top) and parking attendents (bottom).

Far Right: The Huntington Park Casino is one of a handful of legalized card clubs. Players may choose from only three games: draw poker, lo-ball (opposite of draw) and panguingue (similar to gin). The biggest pot at the Casino? $57,000.

Overleaf: Track star Edwin Moses has not lost a 400-meter hurdles race since 1977. The holder of the Olympics record, he expects to rule the roost through the 1988 Seoul Games at least.

BRITAIN HILL

BRITAIN HILL

STEPHEN F. SOMERSTEIN

SCOTT MORGAN

PETER LAVERY

Since the Dodgers moved to Los Angeles from Brooklyn in 1958, the team has managed to weather a variety of controversies while keeping their squeaky-clean image intact. The team has amassed the largest following in baseball and has won the World Series four times since the move to Los Angeles. With the promise of new young players such as Sax, Brock, and Marshall (nicknamed the "Baby Blues"), 1984 looks like another good year. Here they pose in Anaheim Stadium during the pre-season Freeway Series with the American League team, the California Angels.

MARK SHAW

DENNIS FELDMAN

What do kids do for fun on a Friday night in Los Angeles? Some bowl while others head for the Septic Death show at the Cathay de Grande club in Hollywood *(top).*

Right, top: Break dancers on Hollywood Boulevard take a rest from the action while in the San Fernando Valley members of the Zoom Club, a mod association, lock lips.

MARK SHAW

DENNIS FELDMAN

LISA POWERS

MOSHE BRAKHA

The star-making machinery of Los Angeles never shuts down, whether it's Brooke Shields trying on her Bob Mackie-designed Oscar presentation dress *(left)* or a fantasy shoot *(above)*.

Overleaf: There's no doubt about who the star is at the mud wrestling bouts at Hollywood's Tropicana. Cona the Barbarian bellows out her victory cry after vanquishing a challenger. Men often get into the act as well, paying up to $80 for a three-round roll in the mud with a female grappler.

DENNIS KEELEY/DAN BORRIS

BARRY LEWIS

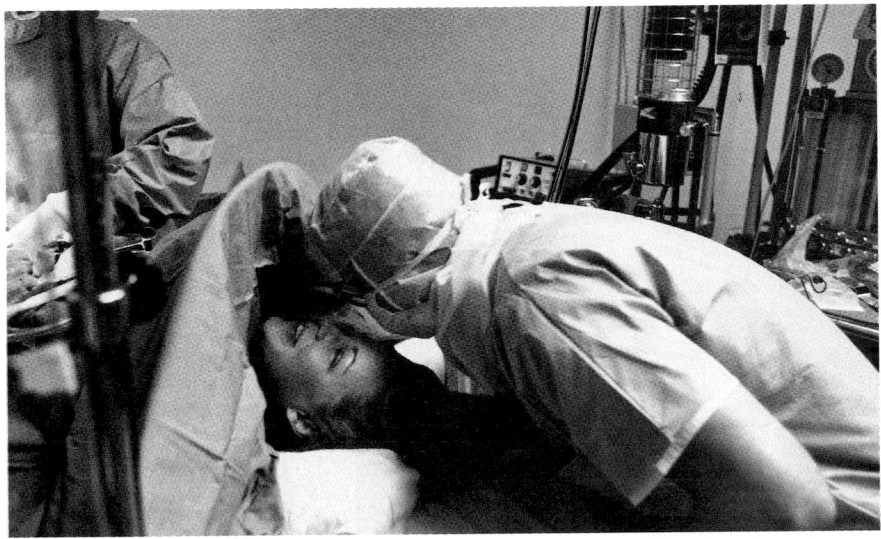

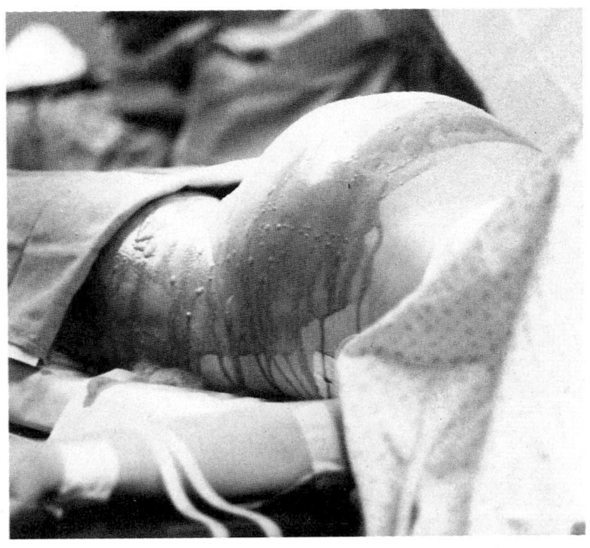

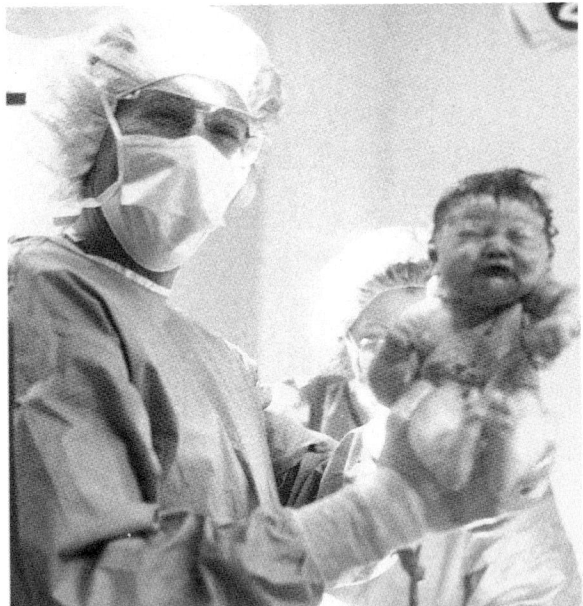

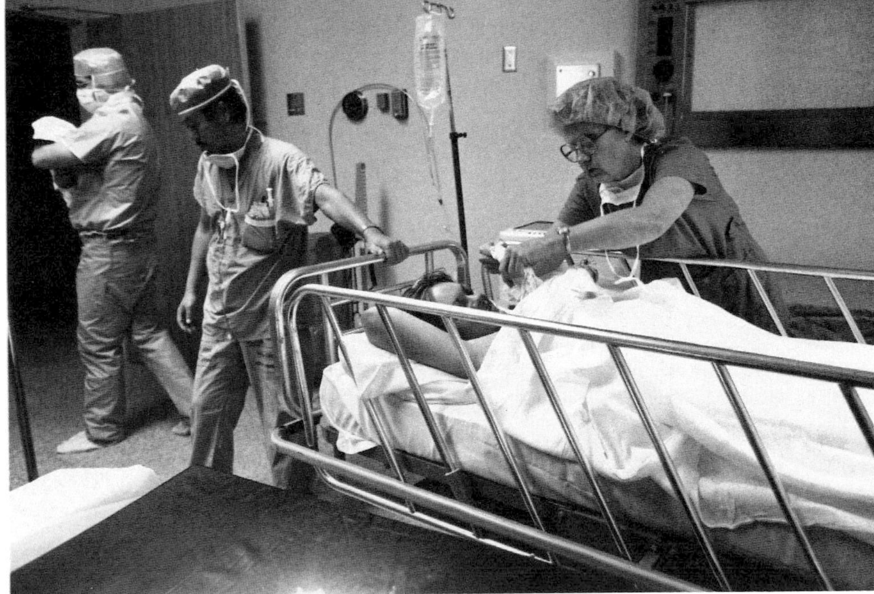

CARROLL BLUE

As paramedics try to help a gunshot victim hold onto life, another life begins in the delivery room of the Santa Monica Hospital. Eight pound Cody Summer Lounsbury arrived by caesarean birth yowling healthily.

Spotlight Tattoo Studio 1983
Spotlite Tattoo
Spotlight Studio
USA

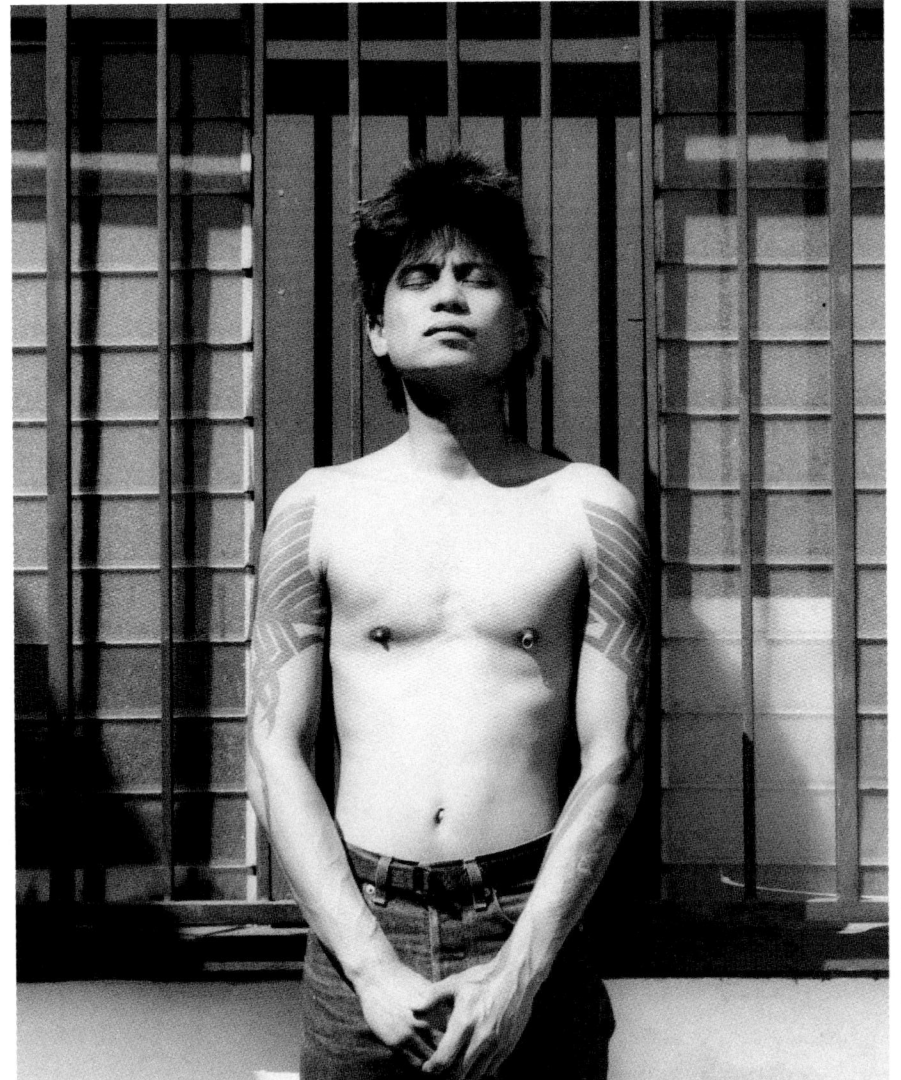

ROBERT MAPPLETHORPE

Tattoos once appealed only to sailors and bikers, but now they draw punks and rock bands, who usually choose band logos over the more usual dragons, tigers, and American bald eagles. "We can duplicate any picture you want," boasted Leo Zuluetta, part-owner of the Spotlite Tattoo Studio in Hollywood.

VOLKER HINZ

"Take it off!" cry hordes of women at Chippendale's beefcake revue in West Los Angeles. Male dancers parade before the all-female audience and strip down to g-string briefs. Ladies clutching dollar bills wave frantically at the dancers, hoping to buy a kiss and tuck their payment into the man's shorts. Sauce for the goose, say some, while others see the sleaze-and-tease as simply another form of commercial sexism.

VOLKER HINZ

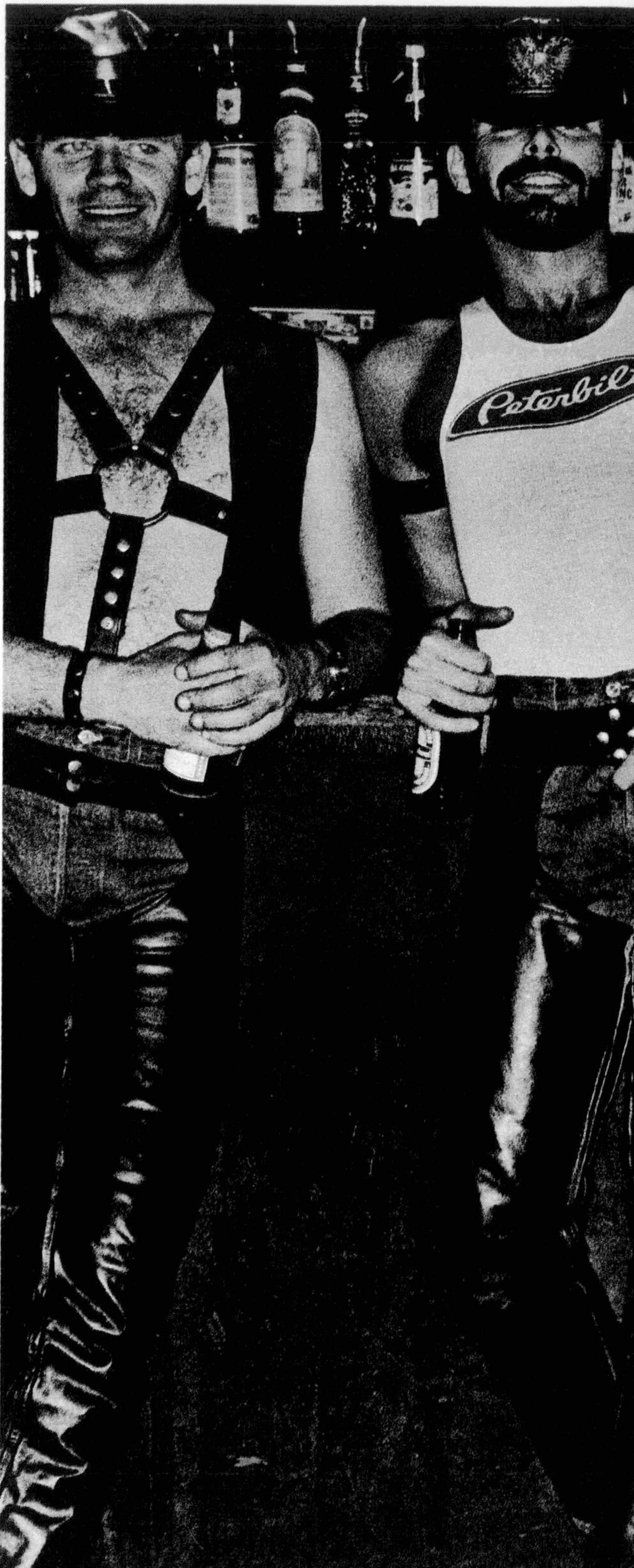

GREGORY CLOUD

The Los Angeles gay and lesbian club scene, says a worker from the Gay Archives, is "more parochial than San Francisco and more reasonable (but not more sensible) than New York." It is estimated that one-third of the bars in Los Angeles cater to the area's one million gays. What is the appeal of clubs such as Probe *(above)* and the Pits *(right)*? "They present an immediate gratification: sexually, socially, and fantasy-wise."

Overleaf: Members of the band Devo at the Entourage restaurant.

RICHARD NOBLE

RAUL VEGA

WILLIAM MIDDLEBROOK

As midnight approaches, the denizens of skid row scramble for a safe place to sleep. With mission beds fully occupied, transients and other homeless people make beds out of cardboard and discarded newspapers in alleyways, parks, doorways, and sidewalks. While police do pick up those who are drunk, they generally let the sleepers alone. Those who can head for the Weingart Detoxification Center where one of the organization's rooms may be rented for eight dollars. "More and more well educated people are turning up," says a spokeswoman. "And a lot of women who have never had a place of their own."

Overleaf: Philanthropist and art collector Dona Powell chairs the board of the Dona Corporation.

HORST WACKERBARTH

WILLIAM KLEIN

JIN YOKOYAMA

A friend on each arm, this computer expert enters Voila in the Beverly Center.

Left, top left: Farewell to fame—it's closing night for Tomata du Plenty's art show at the Zero One club.

Prior page: At a convention of Furniture Manufacturer's of California held at the Sheraton Grande Hotel in downtown.

MARK SHAW

The Club Lingerie in Hollywood has become one of the most popular local watering holes. While the doorman Jason *(above)* picks up some reading material, waitresses pose with the emcee *(top right)* and customers line up .

Far right: Local artists Zacharey and Linda "Tex" Jones.

Overleaf: As the clubs close, the booths at Al's Coffee Shop fill.

GARY LEONARD

MARI UMEKUBO

al's
OPEN 24 HRS
COFFEE SHOP
STEAKS
GUEST PARKING
DONUTS

KEVIN CLARKE

ELSA FLORES

It's been a long and exciting day for *Nuestra Señora la Reina de Los Angeles,* Our Lady, Queen of the Angels. The burdens and joys of her star-struck children have taxed her patience, yet filled her heart with undeniable pride. At last it's time to sleep, as neon gives way to candlelight and dreams of success never ending.

MIKE ABRAHAMS
London, England
Britisher Abrahams shoots for a variety of London publications, including *The Times* (London), *The Sunday Times*, and *The Observer.* He is a graduate of the Polytechnic of Central London and has had his photos exhibited at the Half Moon Gallery.

BILL ARON
Los Angeles, CA
Over the past 10 years, Aron has produced stirring photographic portfolios of Jewish communities in New York, California, Jerusalem, the Soviet Union, and Cuba. *The New York Times Magazine* and *The Village Voice* have published his work. He is represented by these agencies: After Image in Los Angeles, Jeroboam in San Francisco, and Black Star in New York.

LORETTA AYEROFF
Beverly Hills, CA
"Miss Ayerhoff's pictures of men allow her subjects to be themselves in front of the camera; one's admiration goes up and up," says one reviewer of this West Coast freelance photographer's black-and-white exploration of the male mystique. She presently instructs a course in developing a photographic portfolio at the University of California, Los Angeles.

SHERRY RAYN BARNETT
Los Angeles, CA
A photographer who specializes in travel and entertainment imagery, Barnett lists Embassy Television and Chrysalis Records among her many clients. Currently a staff photographer for the *Hollywood Reporter,* she has published nationally since 1970. From Forest Hills, New York, she now lives in Hollywood and is currently involved with television and video productions.

WILFRIED BAUER
Hamburg, Germany
This West German photographer has won international notice for his 35mm pictures. A frequent contributor to *Stern,* Bauer attracted considerable attention for the photo walk he took between Germany and Rome.

ERNESTO BAZAN
New York, NY
Four years after he picked up a camera, this Italian-born photographer had his work published in *Life* magazine. A year later he was a member of Magnum Photos, New York. He received a special prize from the Jury of International Triennial Photopgraphy, Freiburg, West Germany, 1981; first prize in both the Young Photographer Contest, Arles, France, 1981; and the Photo Reportage "News" Contest, 1982, also in Arles.

CARROLL BLUE
Los Angeles, CA
She has been a director, writer, producer, or production assistant on a number of films including "On Golden Pond," "Nine To Five," and "Rollover." Her 1977 film "Two Women," won a number of awards. The same is true of her "Conversations With Roy DeCarava" made for Public Broadcasting Service. Blue is a graduate of the University of California, Los Angeles, and Boston University. For *24 Hours in the Life of Los Angeles,* Blue served as both a photographer and a consultant.

DAN BORRIS
Santa Monica, CA
A Chicago native, Borris now lives in Santa Monica. After graduating from the San Francisco Art Institute with a bachelor's degree in fine arts, he began work in photography. Much of his career has involved video production work for Public Broadcasting Service, Tommy Boy Records, and various independent rock videos. Borris has published his work in the *L.A. Reader* and the *L.A. Weekly.*

MOSHE BRAKHA
Los Angeles, CA
This self-styled "square photographer" says that he was "born in Israel and reborn where Fairfax meets Hollywood Boulevard." A longtime American citizen, Brakha has published in *Esquire, Rolling Stone,* and *Playboy* among many other magazines.

SCOTT BROCK
Los Angeles, CA
An assistant on shoots for *Playboy, Esquire, Camp Graphics,* and for California Kid Productions. About his *24 Hours* experience, the native Californian says it's the "fastest moving and most exciting project I've ever worked on!" With a bachelor of arts degree from the University of California, Los Angeles, film school, Brock continues his education there, working towards his master's .

PATRICK BRUCHET
Paris, France
"Countryside Doctor—Nostalgia of the 50s" was the theme of one of his many exhibits. Bruchet lists *Paris Match* among his many clients and is a native of Angers, France.

RENE BURRI
Paris, France
This cosmopolitan Swiss-born photographer's impressive history has been shaped by the world's trouble spots: 1958, on the eve of a union between Syria and Egypt; 1959, Archbishop Makarios' return to Cyprus after exile; 1963, the burial of John F. Kennedy; 1965, China's industrial revolt; and 1977, the Falkland Islands. His themes are the architectural and the political, how sense of place shapes history and its makers. Burri has published in all the world's great magazines such as *Life, Geo* and *Stern.* His photo-essay, *The Germans*, was published in 1962.

DENNIS CALLWOOD
Los Angeles, CA
His pictures have been published in the books, *A Day In The Life of London* and *Black Women: Achievements Against The Odds* and in *Obscura* magazine. Most notable of his exhibits have been "Alternatives 1980," Ohio University, and "Recent Photographs." Callwood is a member of the Cultural and Fine Arts Advisory Commission to the Los Angeles Olympic Coordinating Committee.

WILL WHITE • DAN BORRIS • DENNIS KEELEY

GUSMANO CESARETTI
Pasadena, CA
This self-taught photographer works in 35mm and has published in *California*, the *Los Angeles Times*, and *Rolling Stone*. His exhibitions include the Fisher Gallery at the University of Southern California and the Los Angeles County Museum of Art. Born in Florence, Italy, Cesaretti now lives in Los Angeles.

KEVIN CLARKE
New York, NY
This graduate in sculpture from Cooper Union School of Art and resident of New York works in 6x7cm and 5x7. His work has appeared in *Life, Stern, Geo*, and *The Times* (London) Supplement. The Photographer's Gallery in London; RZA Gallery, Dusseldorf; Artist's Space, New York; the Kunstverein, Basel; and the Frankfurter Kunstverein have exhibited his pictures.

GREGG CLOUD
Los Angeles, CA
Los Angeles native Cloud studied at the Chouinard Art Institute, Art Center College of Design, and the University of Southern California. Cloud is currently a teacher at the Otis Art Institute of the Parsons School of Design in Los Angeles and free-lances as both a commercial illustrator and a photographer. Cloud has been shooting since 1970 and has had his work exhibited at numerous museums and galleries over the last 10 years.

DENNIS DARLING
Austin, Texas
"Great fun! Let's do it again," said this New York-born photographer about his experience with *24 Hours*. Darling's pictures have graced the pages of *Fortune* and *Esquire*. Currently a journalism professor at the University of Texas, Darling took his undergraduate work at Georgia State University and his master's at the Art Institute of Chicago.

P.L. dICORCIA
New York, NY
From New York City, he taught photography in several universities after graduating from Yale University in 1979. He worked for such magazines as *Fortune, Esquire, Science Digest*, and *Horizon*. He has received grants and awards from the Boston Museum of Fine Arts, the National Endowment for the Arts, and Yale University.

CRAIG DIETZ
Los Angeles, CA
"I was born in Hollywood and it's affected the rest of my life," says photographer Craig Dietz. Obviously his birthplace has not had an adverse effect. Since he graduated from film school at the University of California, Los Angeles, Dietz has enjoyed a career that has included 24 exhibitions, two grants from Polaroid, and appearances in numerous publications ranging from *Time, Artweek, California*, and *Saturday Review* to *The New York Times, The Sunday Times* (London), and the *Los Angeles Times*.

HENRY DILTZ
Los Angeles, CA
Besides having a picture of Paul McCartney on the cover of *Life* magazine, Diltz has contributed to *Rolling Stone* and Germany's *Bravo*, and such books as *Shooting Stars* (Rolling Stone), *California Rock* (Addison House), and *Crosby, Stills, Nash* (St. Martin's Press). Capitol, Columbia, Elektra, Asylum, and Atlantic rank among his impressive list of record company clients. His exhibitions have included a showing at the Museum of Rock Art in Los Angeles.

MIKE DOUD
Los Angeles, CA
Since graduating from Art Center College of Design in 1961, the creative director of *24 Hours In The Life of Los Angeles* has lived and worked in London as art director with various ad agencies and later as art director for A&M Records. He has designed and art-directed hundreds of record covers. His Supertramp's *Breakfast in America* album cover won the Grammy in 1979. Album cover Grammy nominations include Led Zepplin's *Physical Graffiti*, 1975 and Rick Springfield's *Working Class Dog*, 1982.

STEPHANE DuROY
Paris, France
"*24 Hours* is so interesting for me because it is my first time in the U.S.A.," said this 36-year-old member of Rapho Agency. A contributor to *Stern, Geo*, and *Paris Match*, DuRoy's work (35mm) appeared in the *Paris Match* exhibition, 1982.

MITCH EPSTEIN
New York, NY
One of ten American photographers selected for the *Day in the Life of London* project, Epstein also received a Columbia Pictures honorarium to photograph the making of the film *Annie* in 1981. He received a National Endowment for the Arts grant for photography in 1978. His many exhibits include one-man shows at the Light Gallery in New York, and Vision Gallery in Boston.

DAN ESGRO
Los Angeles, CA
Los Angeles is base of operations for Esgro whose accounts span the editorial desk, the corporate world, and advertising. A member of The Image Bank and Imperial Press, Japan, he recently completed a book on the Los Angeles Police.

MARY LLOYD ESTRIN
Los Angeles, CA
Her major publication has been a book of portraits of the very rich, *To The Manor Born*, (the New York Graphic Society). Her work has been shown at Sonnabend in New York; G. Ray Hawkins, Los Angeles; and at Camerawork in San Francisco. Born in Chicago in 1944, Estrin got her bachelor's degree from a University in California, Berkeley, and her master's from the Illinois Institute of Technology. She now lives in Los Angeles.

KLAUS FABRICIUS
London, England
Joint initiator and organizer in *24 Hours in the Life of Los Angeles*, Fabricius runs his own London-based operation where he produces and packages books primarily photographic in nature. He is a consultant to photographers in Europe and North and South America. His particular expertise is the orchestration of book projects, photo exhibitions, and commercial and editorial photo assignments. Born in post-World War II Nuremberg, Fabricius has made England his home since 1975.

BERNARD FALLON
Los Angeles, CA
Liverpudlian Fallon studied graphic design at the Liverpool College of Art. After spending six years as a staff photographer for the London publication *TVTimes*, Fallon moved to the United States. Since then, he has free-lanced for many entertainment and editorial outlets.

PAUL FORTUNE FEARON
Los Angeles, CA
This photographer's one-man shows "Late Show Shadows" (1979) and "L.A.T.V." (1981) were seen in Los Angeles and Tokyo, Japan. Born in Liverpool, Fearon has lived in the United States since 1979. He works with 20x24 Polaroid.

DENNIS FELDMAN
Studio City, CA
Feldman is a native of Washington, D.C. Following graduation from Harvard College, he studied with Walker Evans at Yale in 1971. Pall Press published his book, *American Images*, in 1977. Feldman shoots primarily in 35mm.

KAREN FILTER
Los Angeles, CA
Midwest-born Filter has been a prolific contributor to many magazines including *Playboy, Playgirl, Glamour, Downbeat, California, New York, High Times*, and *PSA*. Her other clients include record companies and advertising agencies. A graduate of the University of California, Los Angeles, and Brooks Institute.

ELSA FLORES
Los Angeles, CA
Significant exhibitions in her blossoming career have included the New Museum, New York, in June 1983; the University of Erlangen, Nuremberg, Germany in January 1983; and California State University, Long Beach, in May 1980. Originally from Las Vegas, Nevada, this Latina artist has published in *Art Week, Art in America, La Opinión* (Los Angeles), and *Nuestro* magazine, among many others.

RENATE von FORSTER
Frankfurt, Germany
"It's a really great idea, I hope to do it again," is von Forster's opinion of *24 Hours*. A member of the Bilderberg photographic agency, von Forster has contributed 35mm photos to *Geo, Stern*, and *Zeit* magazines. Von Forster's pictures have illustrated books such as *Ciudad de los Muchachos*, and *The Tin Drum*.

JOHN FREE
Los Angeles, CA
Nominated for the Pulitzer Prize for his photo-essay on the transients who ride America's freight trains, this native of Tarrytown, New York, got into photography while serving in the United States Marine Corps. Free names Cartier-Bresson and Garry Winogrand among his influences.

GUGLIELMO GALVIN
Dublin, Ireland
"Thank you for having me. Perhaps when I come down I will be able to explain what a mind blowing experience it has all been," says Dublin-born Galvin. He has published in the *Sunday Times* (London), Woman Magazine, The Observer, and many other publications. Galvin also worked on *A Day in the Life of London*.

FRANK GARGANI
Los Angeles, CA
This Philadelphia native says, "I like living in L.A., the weather and the freeways. The way everything is spread out gives me a chance to breathe and to think." His work has appeared in the *L.A. Weekly, Twist, No*, and the *Daily News* Sunday Magazine.

TOBY GLANVILLE
London, England
"Stimulating both culturally and aesthetically," commented this Londoner about *24 Hours*, adding, "I don't want to go home!" He is a contributor to *The Sunday Times* Magazine (London), *The Observer, Ritz*, and *Time Out*. He works in 2¼x2¼.

JERRY GORDON
New York, NY
Gordon's clients range from TWA, ATT, and General Electric to such publications as *Fortune, Forbes, Cuisine*, and *Business Week*. His work has been widely exhibited in the United States and Europe. Now living in New York, Chicago-born Gordon has a master's degree from the Illinois Institute of Technology. He works in 35mm.

TODD GRAY
Los Angeles, CA
This California Institute of the Arts graduate has shown his work in Verona and Milan, Italy, as well as at the Los Angeles County Museum, and the Laguna Beach Museum of Art.
He has been a contributor to *Vogue* (Italy) and *Zoom* (Italy). *Time* magazine, CBS Records, and Warner Records are among his other clients.

MARK HANAUER
Los Angeles, CA
Working on *24 Hours* was "an excellent exercise in pushing myself," says this self-taught photographer. He uses all photographic formats and has contributed to *GQ, Forbes, Fortune, Geo, Rolling Stone, Newsweek, Time, Elle*, and *Moviegoer*. He was born in and resides in Los Angeles.

CHRISTINE HANSCOMB
London, England
Born in Reading, England, and a London resident, Hanscomb has exhibited her work at the National Theatres and Photographers' Gallery (London). Her work has appeared in such food books as *Country Kitchens, Chinese Delights, Healthy Eating*, and *Sunday Times Around The World*. She has also been a contributor to *Vogue, The Sunday Times, Good Housekeeping*, and *The Observer*.

BRITAIN HILL
New York, NY
Born in Rockford, Illinois, Hill now divides her time between New York City and New Hampshire.
She is a contributor to *Fortune, Parade, Newsweek, Maclean's, Ms., The New York Times* Magazine, *Rolling Stone*, and *Moviegoer*.
Her clients range from Polaroid to Warner and A&M Records.
Hill studied at the San Francisco Art Institute and Art Center College of Design in Pasadena, California. Hill prefers shooting in 2¼x2¼.

DOUGLAS HILL
Los Angeles, CA
This London-born photographer has had nine one-man shows and 18 group shows in places as far apart as Hollywood and Zurich. Freelancer Hill worked on the Los Angeles Documentary Project from 1979 to 1981 on a grant from the National Endowment for the Arts. He has published in *Camera* and *Artweek*.

VOLKER HINZ
New York, NY
Born in Hamburg, Hinz now lives in New York. After five years as an aviation mechanic, he served in the German armed forces where he discovered his interest in photography. Hinz then became a freelancer for *Der Spiegel*, *Stern*, and *Die Zeit*. Later he joined Springer's Sven Simon agency and took pictures all over the world. A *Stern* staffer since 1974, he has published work in *Geo*, *Epoca*, *Photo*, *Manchette*, *Life*, *Look*, *Newsweek*, and *Paris Match*.

DAVID HOCKNEY
Los Angeles, CA
Known best for his drawings and paintings, this world famous, award-winning painter, photographer, and Yorkshireman's lists of accomplishments are staggering. Recent among scores of publications featuring work by or on Hockney, are *Images & Issues*, *The Times Literary Supplement* (London), *The New York Times*, and the *San Francisco Camerawork Quarterly*. His impressive group and individual exhibits from 1963 to the present, in the United States, Europe, and around the world, number into the hundreds. The Art Institute of Chicago, The Arts Council of Great Britain, the Solomon R. Guggenheim Museum (New York), and the Museo Tamayo in Mexico City, are a mere few of the many collections in which his work appears.

CURT JOHNSON
Long Beach, CA
"From the busy life of the metropolitan area to the weekend retreat of nature's soothing therapy, I can come back to work with the added interest to record, on film, history in this fascinating field of journalism," says Johnson who arrived in California from Minneapolis 21 years ago to work at the *Long Beach Press Telegram*.

DENNIS KEELEY
Los Angeles, CA
Living and working in Los Angeles, Keeley has published in *California*, *Rolling Stone*, the *L.A. Weekly*, and the *L.A. Reader*. His one-man shows include the California Institute of the Arts, 1975 and the Los Angeles County Museum of Art rental gallery. A resident of Los Angeles, Keeley works in 2¼x2¼.

RON KELLEY
Santa Monica, CA
His monograph, *Yemenis of the San Joaquin* and his publications in the *Los Angeles Times*, *After Image*, and *Scree* magazine indicate his diverse interests. He has exhibited his 35mm work at LACE (Los Angeles Contemporary Exhibitions), the 8th Street Gallery, and the Los Angeles Center for Photographic studies. Kelley studied anthropology at Michigan State University and cinema at the University of California, Los Angeles.

BASIA KENTON
Santa Monica, CA
Born in Warsaw and now living in Los Angeles, Kenton went to school in Warsaw, Moscow, London, and Rome before studying photography at Santa Monica College and the University of California, Los Angeles. Her pictures have appeared in *Artweek*, the *L.A. Weekly*, *American Film*, *Images & Issues*, *Petersen's Photographic*, and *Vanguard*. Exhibits of her work have been held at the Los Angeles Center for Photographic Studies.

WILLIAM KLEIN
Paris, France
A self-styled revolutionary with camera, Klein is both blessed and cursed as recent history's most radical photographer. *Eldridge Cleaver, Black Panther*, *Mr. Freedom*, and *Far From Vietnam*, are three of his best known films; and *Rome* (1960), *Moscow* (1964), *Tokyo* (1964), and his native *New York* (1964), are four of several self-designed Klein books. A social sciences major at City University of New York, who later studied at the Sorbonne in Paris; and former fashion photographer for Alexander Liberman at *Vogue* magazine, Klein has had world-wide exhibits of his work and received honors such as the Prix Nadar, Paris.

ROBERT LANDAU
Los Angeles, CA
Among his 18 exhibitions are one-man shows in the Galeria Aglaia, Florence; the Leopold Gold Gallery, Santa Monica; the Mancini Gallery, Houston; the Palm Springs Desert Museum, California; and the New Media Gallery, Ventura, California. His work has appeared in *Art in America*, *Geo*, *Artweek*, *Graphis*, *Horizon*, *New West*, *Zoom*, *Newsweek*, *Rolling Stone*, *Wet*, and *Los Angeles*.

VICTOR LANDWEBER
Los Angeles, CA
This photographer's productive scope encompasses over 20 exhibitions in the United States and abroad. Landweber also publishes limited edition portfolios of original prints by well-known photographers. *Victor Landweber Photographs, 1967-1984* by J. Hugunin, was a catalog for the Museum of Photographic Arts, San Diego, 1984.

PETER LAVERY
London, England
In between advertising shoots and editorial work for *The Sunday Times*, Londoner Lavery spends his time documenting European circus life. A graduate of the Royal College of Art, London.

RON LEIGHTON
Laguna Beach, CA
This highly successful photographer proudly points to his photographs in a book published by the G. Ray Hawkins Gallery, Los Angeles, in 1976. Although born in New York, Leighton is an alumnus of California State University, Fullerton, and presently lives in Laguna Beach.

GARY LEONARD
Los Angeles, CA
He has exhibited his 35mm photographs at California State University, Los Angeles and LACE (Los Angeles Contemporary Exhibitions) as well as at the Zero Zero and the Lhasa clubs. His photos have appeared in the *L.A. Weekly* and the *L.A. Reader*.

ELISA LEONELLI
Los Angeles, CA
She has contributed to many publications including *Us*, *People*, *TV Guide*, the *Los Angeles Times*, *Zoom*, and *Westways* in the United States, and *Europeo*, *Grazia*, *Amica*, and *Uomo Vogue* in Italy. Leonelli has exhibited in Galeria Comunale, Modena, Italy, and at the Lhasa Club in Los Angeles. Leonelli spent five years with ABC Television and has taught at Otis Art Institute of the Parsons School of Design.

BARRY LEWIS
London, England
A contributor to *The Observer*, *Geo*, *Newsweek*, *Radio Times* and others, this photographer has a degree in

chemistry as well as photography. He has exhibited his work at the Photographer's Gallery (London) and the Museum of London. He participated in the *Day in the Life of London* project.

ROMAN LEZO
Sherman Oaks, CA
A native of Czechoslovakia, Lezo has built a solid career in the United States. His photos have been published in a wide variety of journals. Lezo's most recent exhibited work was in the Photo Show International in 1984 in Las Vegas. His comments about the *24 Hours* project: "I was racing against the clock. It was a challenge to capture in color the 'not so fancy' areas of Los Angeles."

JOHN LONDEI
London, England
Largely an advertising photographer, Londei has spent the past nine years traveling the British Isles photographing disappearing, old picturesque shops, and other civilized refinements succumbing to the technological march of time in 20th century England. He participated in the *Day in the Life of London* project.

KEVIN LYNCH
Los Angeles, CA
Inspired by Horst Wackerbarth in Frankfurt, Lynch has worked as a freelance assistant on his very intense project, "The Red Couch, an American Epic" for the past four years both in Germany and in the United States. Born in Chicago, Lynch was raised and educated in Paris, Belgium, and Germany. He presently works as a freelance photographer in Los Angeles.

CHRISTOPHER MAKOS
New York, NY
A graduate of the University of Southern California and a former student of artist Man Ray, Makos has exhibited extensively in both America and Europe. His numerous credits cover both continents, ranging from *The New York Times* to *Esquire, The Village Voice, L'Uomo-Vogue,* and *Blueboy.* He served as art director on Andy Warhol's book *Exposures.* Makos currently lives in New York.

GERED MANKOWITZ
London, England
"Just about" educated in photography, to use his own words, this photographer found his work on *24 Hours In the Life of Los Angeles* "very exciting and stimulating." A native of London, England, Mankowitz has been featured in many publications including *The Sunday Times* (London), *The Observer, Time Out, Harpers & Queen,* and *Tatler.* "Pop Portraits," his most successful exhibit to date, was on display at the Photographers' Gallery in London.

ROBERT MAPPLETHORPE
New York, NY
"Black Males," "Lady Lisa Lyon", and "Portraits of Patti Smith" are only three distinguished exhibits by this prolific New York photographer. The Jane Corking Gallery in Toronto; the Centre Georges Pompidou, Paris; the Olympus Centre, London; the Gallery Watari, Tokyo; and the Institute of Contemporary Art, London, are among the more recent galleries that have exhibited the artistry of this luminary of the photographic world.

PETER MARTENS
Rotterdam, Holland
Holland's 1983 Photographer of The Year, Martens received his education at the Dutch School of Photography in The Hague. He participated in *A Day in the Life of London* and presently has a color exhibit of his work in Amsterdam, and an exhibit of black and white photographs in Rotterdam.

NORMAN MAUSKOPF
Pasadena, CA
Mauskopf began his second career in 1980 after studying at the Art Center College of Design. Mauskopf has shot for a variety of organizations and *California* and *Los Angeles* magazines. He is a member of the Advertising Photographers of America as well as the Professional Rodeo Cowboys Association. Currently he is at work on a black and white study of the American rodeo cowboy.

PAUL MAXON
Los Angeles, CA
He started out in 1978 as a studio manager and assistant for Tom Weihs in New York. In 1979 he free-lanced as both a designer and photographer for a variety of companies. Maxon then went on to work as the staff designer/photographer for Hipgnosis Design of London. Now based in Hollywood.

KENNETH McGOWAN
Los Angeles, CA
His photos have appeared in *Art Forum, Vanity Fair, Vogue, Zoom,* and *Rolling Stone.* Originally from Ogden, Utah, McGowan moved to California at the age of 20. His work can be found in the collections of the Metropolitan Museum of Art, New York; Fogg Art Museum, Harvard; Cornell University; the Museum of Modern Art, New York; and the National Archives.

VINCENT MENTZEL
Rotterdam, Holland
A native of Holland, Mentzel has contributed to *Newsweek, The Sunday Times* (London), and other publications. Mentzel's photos of life in rural china and Tibet are on exhibit at Museum Boymans van Beuningen in Rotterdam. Mentzel is a graduate of Rotterdam's Academy of Fine Arts.

WILLIAM MIDDLEBROOK
Compton, CA
"I have an overwhelming urge to make a statement about being black, to express the joy, also to portray the negative, the truth from which there's no escape," says this Detroit-born photographer.

REID MILES
Los Angeles, CA
This photographer-illustrator recreates the simpler time of pretelevision America in the style of Norman Rockwell. "Design is everything. I am really an art director," declares Chicago-born Miles. After living for some time in New York, he moved to California where he "began to see people as other than props."

ANDREW MOORE
New York, NY
"A 24-hour coffee highway freeway boulevard burnout!" is the way photographer Moore describes his *24 Hours* experience. A Princeton University alumnus, Connecticut-born Moore now resides in New York City. His work may be found in the Seagram Collection and at the Princeton University Art Museum.

SCOTT MORGAN
Los Angeles, CA
This Maryland native comes to photography with training in painting and sculpture at the University of California, Santa Barbara as well as in photography at Orange Coast College. His work was included in Orange Coast College's Group Show in 1979 and in a show at the Los Angeles Institute of Contemporary Art in 1980.

MELANIE NISSEN
Sunland, CA
This native Angeleno has seen her work in *Slash, Wet, High Performance, Stuff, Mademoiselle, Chic, Art Direction,* and various "fanzines" throughout Europe and the United States. Nissen called *24 Hours* "the best assignment ever."

RICHARD NOBLE
Los Angeles, CA
A photographer who enjoys doing editorial and journalistic assignments as a means to expand his creative horizons, Noble has nevertheless chosen advertising photography as his main career. A contributor to *GQ, Esquire, Look, Redbook, Venture,* and *Ladies' Home Journal,* to name a few.

GREG O'LOUGHLIN
Glendale, CA
This 22-year old photographer is currently involved in studying commercial photography and has spent the past six years making sand sculptures. O'Loughlin studied at the Art Center College of Design, Pasadena.

AVE PILDAS
Los Angeles, CA
In his 34 years as a professional, Pildas has worked as a designer, professor, art director, and freelance photographer. Many know his work through his two highly acclaimed books, *Art Deco Los Angeles* and *Movie Palaces.*

LISA POWERS
Los Angeles, CA
Specializing in fashion, advertising, record covers, and celebrities, Powers lives and works in the Hollywood Hills. She has been a contributor to *Vogue, Mademoiselle, Glamour, Cosmo, GQ, Oui, Wet, Harper's Bazaar* (Italy), and many more.

ANDREJ REISER
Hamburg, Germany
A frequent contributor to *Stern, Geo, Ambiente,* and *FAZ,* as well as to the books *Paris* by Hoffman and Campe, and *Ostfriesland* by Schwalfeld, Reiser is a member of the Bilderberg Photo Agency. Born in Czechoslovakia, he presently makes his home in Hamburg, where he occasionally exhibits his work.

PETER REISS
Los Angeles, CA
Using a 4x5 camera with a pinhole lens, Reiss has won awards and grants repeatedly over the last four years. A cum laude graduate in psychology, he has worked as a photo instructor for numerous institutions in Los Angeles, including Otis Art Institute of the Parsons School of Design; the University of California, Los Angeles; the University of Southern California.

BARRIE ROKEACH
Kensington, CA
With a bachelor's in math and a master's in design/photography from the University of California, Berkeley, Rokeach has made a name for himself in aerial photography. A resident of Kensington (near San Francisco), Rokeach said about the *24 Hours* project, "Crazy city, crazy project, crazy bunch of shooters."

DELLA ROSSA
Los Angeles, CA
Capturing the ethnic diversity of Los Angeles has been the trademark of this long-time resident. Her remarkable street-wise sensibilities have produced striking images for nearly 20 years. Her subjects have ranged from extensive coverage of the 1965 Watts riots to a recent photo essay on poverty in the *barrio* for a local newspaper.

MARISSA ROTH
Los Angeles, CA
A woman with clearly defined goals, Roth hopes to obtain recognition and success as a photographer and designer "to demonstrate through my work the world as I see it." A contributor to *Flare,* and *Women's Wear Daily.*

RED SAUNDERS
London, England
Project director of *24 Hours in the Life of Los Angeles,* his influences range from Soviet contructivist Rodchenko to New York photographer Diane Arbus. English by birth, Saunders has worked for many publications including *Rolling Stone, Esquire, Fortune,* and *The Sunday Times* (London). His work has taken him all over the world. After being joint conceptualizer/organizer with Syd Shelton in *A Day in the Life of London,* Saunders clearly knows what sort of shot is essential. "We're passionate about reestablishing the primacy and popularity of the single image in the face of all this press-button video garbage."

JEFFREY SCALES
Los Angeles, CA
Since his graduation from the San Francisco Art Institute, Scales has touched on various aspects of the entertainment and communications world. He has worked as a tour manager for major rock and roll artists, as an assistant television producer and director, and as a photo editor for the *L.A. Weekly.* Currently, he is freelancing fulltime, contributing photos to *Rolling Stone, Ms., California, Los Angeles, The Village Voice,* and the *L.A. Reader.*

STEVE SCHAPIRO
Beverly Hills, CA
When asked to list his credits, this photographer replied, "Which ones? You name it. Except for China, I think I've hit them all."

Schapiro did the pictures for *Jane Fonda's Workout Book* and extensive coverage of such films as *Midnight Cowboy, Shampoo,* and *The Great Gatsby.* Affiliated with the Gamma Liaison agency, Schapiro has had his photos featured on the covers of nearly all major publications.

CAROL SCHWALBERG
Los Angeles, CA
This New York expatriate is the author of three books, *From Cattle to Credit Cards, Light and Shadow,* and *Doing It,* as well as over 200 magazine articles. Schwalberg has reviewed photography exhibits for *The Village Voice,* and her 35mm photographs have appeared in *American Way, Popular Photography,* and *Playbill.*

BOB SEIDEMANN
Los Angeles, CA
After having gotten his start as an assistant in New York photographic studios, Seidemann moved to San Francisco in the 60's. There he produced his classic portraits of rock and roll legends Janis Joplin and The Grateful Dead. Later, in London, his cover for Eric Clapton's *Blind Faith* made rock-culture history.

MARK SHAW
Los Angeles, CA
"Since 1979 I have been shooting material for several extended photo documentaries," says this Southern California photographer, "including 100 black and white photographs for an intended monograph on Los Angeles punk rockers." Shaw is also a contributor to the *Los Angeles Times,* the *Los Angeles Herald Examiner,* and *Penthouse.*

JACK SHEAR
Los Angeles, CA
"Things change. I look forward to viewing these images in 2019," says this San Fernando Valley native. Shear has been a contributor to many publications including the *Los Angeles Times,* the *Los Angeles Herald Examiner,* the *L.A. Reader, Artweek,* and *Rolling Stone.* His pictures can be found in numerous private collections.

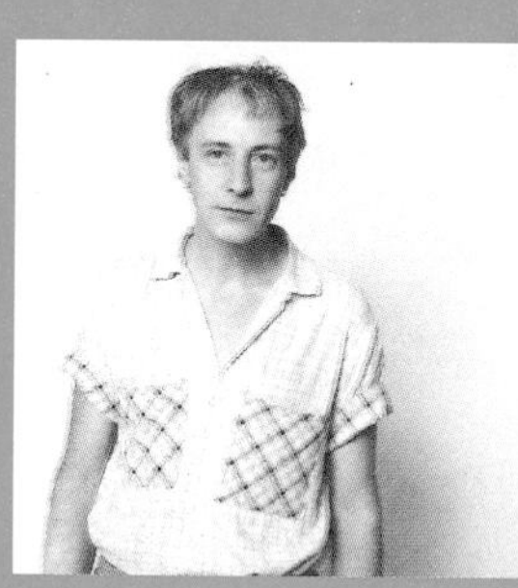

SYD SHELTON
Sydney, Australia
Joint conceptualizer-organizer with Red Saunders and art director on *A Day in the Life of London,* which is to be published in the Fall of 1984, Shelton was born in Yorkshire, England, where he studied painting in art school. He subsequently spent several years teaching painting in London. Shelton has passed the last 10 years working as a free-lance photographer and designer in London and Sydney, where he now lives.

STEPHEN SOMERSTEIN
Laguna Beach, CA
24 Hours was "off the beaten track of what I normally do," Somerstein says, but it was also a "great demand on one's creative talents." Primarily a documentary photographer, Somerstein covered many of the civil rights demonstrations during the 60s including the historic march on Washington. This resident of Laguna Beach, California, resumed his camera work recently after a hiatus of several years.

LOU STOUMEN
Los Angeles, CA
For over 50 years Stoumen has been "an obsessive street photographer." He has worked on four continents, held one-man shows in over 20 cities, published seven books and portfolios, and had 42 of his pictures placed into the collection of New York's Museum of Modern Art. His most recent book, *Times Square—1940 Till Now,* is set for release in 1985.

TIM STREET-PORTER
Los Angeles, CA
Although a native of England, Street-Porter has become well known for his captivating landscape and architectural photos of his adopted home, Los Angeles. His American credit list includes such publications as *House & Garden, California, The New York Times, Vanity Fair,* and *Vogue.* His work has also appeared in Japan's *Brutus,* Italy's *Domus,* and London's *Sunday Times.*

TED TAMADA
Arcadia, CA
Born in Honolulu, Tamada attended the Art Center College of Design (Pasadena) and Pasadena City College. He is a graduate of California State University, Los Angeles, a photography consultant and freelance photographer.

JOSHUA TOUSTER
Santa Monica, CA
A graduate of the Rhode Island School of Design and Evergreen State College in Washington, Touster has taught at the University of Southern California, Woodbury University, and West Los Angeles College.

PIERRE TOUTAIN
Paris, France
Toutain, a native of Normandy, has traveled all over the globe on assignments for such publications as *Stern, Paris Match, Time,* and *Le Figaro.* Photos from tours to Vietnam and Kampuchea were included in a striking exhibition of "Children in The War." He participated in the *Day in the Life of London* project.

ARTHUR TRESS
New York, NY
According to Tress, the photographer is "a being possessed of special powers that enable him to control mysterious forces. He often works in trance-like states." Tress' books include *The Dream Collector,* 1972; *Shadow; A Novel in Photographs,* 1975; *The Theatre of the Mind,* 1976.

JAY ULLAL
Hamburg, Germany
Born in Mangalore, India, and currently a resident of West Germany, Ullal has exhibited his work in Delhi, Bombay, and Hamburg. Ullal graduated in 1953 from the Motion Picture Arts Academy in Bombay. About the *24 Hours in the Life of Los Angeles* project, Ullal volunteered these comments: "Great city. It has various faces and different cultures like Mexicans, Jews, Krishna-Hindu-Sikhs, etc., etc."

MARISSA ROTH

BARRY LEWIS

ACKNOWLEDGEMENTS:

MARTINA BAKO
KLARA BERG
MAYOR TOM BRADLEY
CHRISTIANE BRUESTEDT
LORRAINE BULL
DENNIS CALLWOOD
KEVIN CLARKE
SANDI CAMARA
(Hyatt Hotel,
Sunset Blvd.)
MICHAEL CONNOLLY
DONNA DELANEY
(Kodak Processing,
Las Palmas St.)
HOWARD DEUTSCH
DOS BURRITOS
(Hollywood Blvd.)
JOHN ELLIS
FOCUS FOTO FINISHERS
(black and white printing)
FOTEK PHOTO LAB
(color printing)
FROLIC ROOM
(Hollywood Blvd.)
KATHY GALLAGHER
GARTNER GRAPHICS
(position stats)
LUCIA GILL
HOWARD GOLDSOBEL
CLAUDIA HANCHETT
G. RAY HAWKINS GALLERY
HIGHLAND GARDENS
HOTEL
ROGER JEFFERIES
ALICE FAIRFAX-JONES
DENNIS KEELEY
THEO LAMBERLIN
EDDIE LEIER
(Midway Rent-A-Car)
JAY LEVIN
LOS ANGELES FIRE DEPT.
LOS ANGELES
POLICE DEPT.
MANN'S CHINESE THEATER
MARGAUX MERKIN
(Merkin International's
Drive-A-Dream)
MERRITT TRAVEL
DAVID MILLER
LORI MILLER
(Greater Los Angeles
Visitors Bureau)
MARSHA MOHR
MUSSO & FRANK GRILL
(famous since 1919)
NICK'S PLACE
(for the constant supply
of fine burgers)
IRWIN PEARLMAN
GLENN & LEE PERRY
PETER & SHIRLEY PESSL
ROBERT L. PINCUS
VICTORIA PIPKIN
(Mayor's office)
KAREN SHACKMAN
UNIVERSAL CITY TOURS
Location courtesy of
Universal City Studios, Inc.
HEDI VALENCISE
HORST WACKERBARTH
MICHAEL WALTON
MIKE YAMAMOTO
ZERO-ONE GALLERY
WALTHER ZIMMER

MARI UMEKUBO
Gardena, CA
Although still a student at the time of her participation in the *24 Hours* project, Umekubo obviously knows what to look for in her hometown. Umekubo has attended the Art Center College of Design and graduated from Otis Art Institute of the Parsons School of Design in May 1984, with a bachelor's degree in communication design. While she has worked primarily as a designer thus far in her career, Umekubo has had her photos exhibited at Otis/Parsons and at other local galleries. For the next two years she plans to continue her studies in photography.

RAUL VEGA
Los Angeles, CA
After having attended the schools of architecture at California Polytechnic State University, San Luis Obispo, and the University of Florence, this native Californian began his career as a photographer. Now a resident of Los Angeles, Vega has had his work published in *Time*, *Rolling Stone*, and *Esquire*.

TOM VINETZ
Santa Monica, CA
Beaux Arts, *Images and Issues*, and *Architectural Record* are among the magazines which have published the work of this Los Angeles-born photographer. He attended the University of California, Berkeley, but received his bachelor of arts degree from the University of California, Los Angeles.

HORST WACKERBARTH
Frankfurt, Germany
Readers of *Stern*, *Life*, *Vogue* and *The Sunday Times* (London) are familiar with Wackerbarth's work. A native of Germany, Wackerbarth has exhibited throughout Europe with shows in London, Milan, and Dusseldorf.

E. K. WALLER
Los Angeles, CA
Detroit native Waller has published photos in *New West*, *Redbook*, *Spinning Off* and other publications. In regard to her *24 Hours* experience, Waller remarked: "*24 Hours* was the most exciting and challenging assignment for me yet! I wish every day were as exciting!"

ROBERT WALTER
New York, NY
Editorial director of Alfred van der Marck Editions which he helped found in 1982, Walter is the editor of Joseph Campbell's four-volume *Historical Atlas of World Mythology*. Walter came to publishing after an extensive career in the professional theater both on Broadway and throughout the United States and Canada.

WILLIAM WEGMAN
New York, NY
One of the few photographers in the world to shoot 20x24 Polaroids, Wegman has exhibited his work at the Freedman Gallery in Reading, Pennsylvania; the Holly Solomon Gallery in New York; and the University of Regina, Saskatchewan, Canada. The National Endowment for the Arts awarded him a grant for photography in 1982, and Walker Art Center published a book of his work, *Man's Best Friend*.

LARRY WILLIAMS
New York, NY
"Mildly extensive" is the laid-back fashion in which this New York-based photographer describes the number of his exhibitions, preferring to focus on his contributions to *Rolling Stone*, *Esquire*, *New York*, *House & Garden*, *The Observer*, and *Mademoiselle* magazines among others.

VAL WILMER
London, England
Wilmer is a London photographer who has contributed frequently to radical left, feminist, and music publications in England. She graduated from the Regent Street Polytechnic School of Photography and has had her work published in *The Observer*, *New Musical Express*, and *City Limits* among others. The world of jazz is one of her favorite subjects and was the object of an exhibit "Jazz Seen: The Face of Black Music" (exhibited at the Victoria and Albert Museum in London)

LINDA WOLF
Santa Monica, CA
In 1983 her series of photographic murals of bus riders graced vehicles and bus benches throughout Los Angeles. This year visitors to Los Angeles can see her billboards, "L.A. Welcomes the World," which Eastman Kodak sponsored. She is a graduate of l'Ecole Experimentale Photographique as well as l'Institut Americain, both in France.

JAMES B. WOOD
Los Angeles, CA
This Hollywood resident has contributed to many publications including *Popular Photography*, *Life*, and *Zoom*. His work has been exhibited both in this country and abroad, most notably at the prestigious Nikon Gallery in Tokyo's Ginza district.

JIN YOKOYAMA
Tokyo, Japan
Formerly an assistant to fashion photographer Toshi Takeuchi. Tokyo and Sydney have been bases of operation for this international photographer who moved to the United States in early 1984.

LLOYD ZIFF
New York, NY
A graduate of Pratt Institute in New York, Ziff has worked extensively as both a photographer and an art director. His photos have appeared in *Interview*, *New West*, *Rolling Stone*, and *House & Garden*.

PHOTOGRAPHIC ASSISTANTS:

Joan Borgman
Teri Brown
Jan Butchofsky
Irene Cancel
Irene-Marie Carlson
Carol Cetrone
Laura Davis
Lucy Eidenbock
John Evans
Rubin Figueroa
Michael Fleming
Barry Franenberg
Paul Gadson
Marie Paule Goislard
Tina Midori Imahara
Laura Davis Jaoui
Orden Jones
Raymond Kwan
Mark Leisgarten
Alexandra Lezo
Roman John Lezo
Gerard McLeod
Willow Mahakian
Laura Marenzi
Daniel Marlos
Edward Maxey
William Meade
Rick Mendoza
Jean Mitchel
Michael Nadeau
Jason Neu
Ara Nuyujukian
Theresa Osante
Teresa Plaza
Asher Price
Debbie Richardson
Lara Rossignol
Mario Savvides
Harold Sweet
Suzanne Titus
Penny Venters
Nabil Wassif
Keith Watson
Will White
Carlton Wilkinson
James C.W. Young
David Zaitz